# YOU CAN BLAME IT ON MIKE!

## POLITICAL UPDATES BY MARVIN KLEIN
## THE EARLY YEARS (2004-2005)

# MARVIN KLEIN

Designed By:

**R2 MEDIA GROUP PUBLICATIONS**
*A division of R2 Media Group*
PO Box 4357 Pocatello, ID 83205
www.r2mg.com

ISBN 13: 978-1-5001397-4-2
ISBN 10: 1-5001397-4-2

Printed in the United States of America.

# YOU CAN BLAME IT
# ON MIKE!

POLITICAL UPDATES BY MARVIN KLEIN
THE EARLY YEARS (2004-2005)

## MARVIN KLEIN

# Table of Contents

# Introduction

Take a trip with me back to 2004 to relive the controversial political climate in our country. Republican President George Bush, our war President, is riding high toward reelection in November, while 10 Democrats are hard at work to win the nomination of their party.

After a tough battle, John Kerry won the nomination and then the exciting debates and political battles are off and running.

When we get to the November election, George Bush wins but his percentage margin in the popular vote was the narrowest ever for an incumbent president. And like the election before, it was an amazing campaign that set the tone for future political battles and controversies that we are involved in today.

My Updates were meant to be an enjoyable and educational commentary on this period of our nation's history. Many of our Updaters (readers) disagreed with some or maybe many of my commentaries and that is good because we all learn when we communicate. But for now I hope these Updates will allow you to recall and relive the thoughts you had during those tumultuous years.

Because now, ten years later, our nation is in a similar political turmoil...2014 is not a Presidential Election year but it is filled with critical election campaigns. It is a good time to recall and learn from our experience in 2004 and 2005…the years these Updates cover.

On a personal note, Mike Royko's untimely death is the reason I started to write these commentaries, but now they are in your hands and… like it or not… educational or entertaining, accurate or imaginary, here we go with… *The Political Updates from Marvin for 2004 and 2005.*

And of course, please remember, if you don't like them… Blame it on Mike.

# In the Beginning

## JANUARY 10, 2004

In this exciting political campaign I know you were all waiting for my "inside information" so here it is as we head into the exciting Iowa Caucus. Since I am supporting Gen. Clark Iowa plays a big role in my campaign strategy especially since he is not running in Iowa. The first step is for Dean to win big in Iowa (Clark does not pull any votes away from him). Then Gephardt would probably drop out. Clark has had the money and time to impact New Hampshire but here again I hope Dean wins with Clark second. With this embarrassing loss Kerry will drop out.

Then Lieberman, Kucinich and Braun leave about the same time (pressure from the "Stop Dean Wing" of the party) leaving Dean, Edwards and Clark. Edwards probably hopes to be VP with either of them so he might stay on until someone offers him a deal, but in a field of three Clark has a great chance to win many primaries it will be half a vote for Clark and half a vote against Dean.

Clark picks a VP like Gephardt or some experienced senator so that it "looks like" they know what to do on all foreign and domestic matters and it is on to November.

Then the election will not be Clark against Bush, but rather a referendum on the President and here again Clark has a great chance since it seems the war and economy may continue to be big problems for the country. Clark again is the alternative candidate and he gets all the Gore votes from the last election but wins one or two more states like Florida. It's Hail to the new Chief time.

It's all simple.

Aren't you glad I told you what is going to happen?

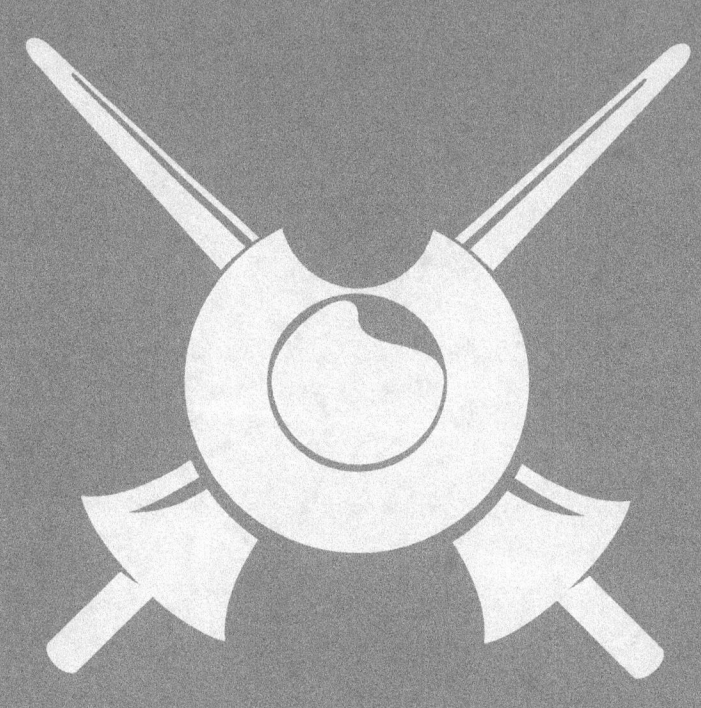

# The Primaries

## CONGRATULATIONS AND THANK YOU IOWA
## JANUARY 18, 2004

The intelligence and devotion of the Iowa voter has electrified the country. It has embarrassed people from both parties and from all states to study and understand the political process. Most important it has attracted young people and drop outs from the political process to get involved an important key for a democracy where only 50% of the people care enough to spend a half hour to vote every four years and for this we have to credit Dean. Amazingly, the Iowa Caucus seems to have had a major impact on all the Democratic Candidates, they are thinking clearer, speaking better and working harder. The country will be the winner no matter who wins in November.

I am still hoping for Gephardt to drop out this week to pave the way for a Clark victory next week, but in any event the higher caliber debate will encourage Bush to be a better President as he begins to sense that the election will be a battle.

## WHAT A NIGHT
## JANUARY 20, 2004

What a night. Iowa exploded with independence, good thinking and excitement. They will be studying the results for years. In any event Dean lost the caucus and then committed suicide with his version of a political war cry. Edwards secured his VP nomination. Now the battle is between Clark and Kerry for the nomination. 50% of the caucus voters were first timers and they were serious political analysts looking for the candidate who can win. New Hampshire will not be decisive. But the voters in South Carolina are going to have an amazingly difficult choice. Sharpton will confuse the results, as I am sure many Black voters will vote for him out of respect. Watch out for a political deal and Sharpton could be a king maker if he throws his support to Kerry or Clark. He is in a position of power that won't be worth much in two months. Edwards as a son of the South will certainly do well the real question is how bad Kerry will do. If he doesn't excite the voters to vote for a traditional northern liberal, than the Democratic voters around the country will turn to Clark as the one who matches up best with the President. Clark just has to remain cool and stay on message can't get into a pissing match like Gephardt and Dean did last week.Hold on to your hats, it is going to be fun.


## THE FEW WHO WILL CHOOSE
## JANUARY 25, 2004

Lot of excitement over who will be the Democratic candidate polls are taken by the hour and millions are being spent on advertising. But the simple fact is that a small number of voters in few states will be making the decision in 2004.The rest of the states are locked up in the Democratic or Republican column unless something unusual happens.

First a little review of 2000. The voters were split between Gore and Bush with a few special interest issues like abortion, and candidates like Nader siphoning enough votes in states like Florida (Nader got almost 100,000 and Bush won by 500) to give Bush the victory.

Since I am hoping for a Democrat to win, we need to focus on those swing states (West Virginia, Arizona, Ohio, Florida, etc.) and determine who are the voters and how can we get their support. The potential Democratic voters fall into five categories.

1. *Let's start with the easy one. "Anyone but Bush Democrats" They didn't like Bush last time and since he has spit in their face for three years they will vote for Mickey Mouse if he can beat Bush. We don't need to cater to them as they are voting against Bush rather than for anyone.*

2. *The next group is also easy. The Green Nader people. They are still hiding for their idealistic vote for Nader and this time will vote for the major parties with the Democrats getting 3 out of 4 votes. Don't worry about Nader, running again if he does he will need bodyguards to attend his own Green Party meetings. But the Democrats must present a strong "Green Message."*

3. *The Flag and God voters are the key in many of these swing states they support the war in Iraq and are very proud Americans. Military figures and images are reassuring to them. Many of these voters also fear liberal candidates. So it is easy to see that Clark (Four Star General from Arkansas) has a chance to win at least a small percentage of them. But more about that later.*

4. *The Lost Battalion. The largest group, who didn't vote for Gore, didn't bother to vote for anyone. They are a major problem in a democracy, but remember people change when they are under intense emotional pressure. My guess is that more will show up in November (unless it conflicts with reruns of "My Big Fat Fiancée) and will have determined the president has something to do with their future.*

*Probably the ones who lost good paying jobs or the college graduates who can't get a good job will find time to vote. Much of this vote should go to the Democrats. Dean showed that he could get some of these folks involved as we saw from the high vote count in Iowa and the party has to learn from him.*

5. *Finally, the last group. The ones our Founding Fathers had in mind when they wrote the Constitution the Independent Voter. Maybe 5% of the electorate. They are looking for intelligent programs, fiscal responsibility, and character of the candidate. The events of the world may decide their vote. If things go well they will stick with Bush, but they are independent and will watch Iraq, the economy, listen to everyone, decide and vote. Our programs have to make sense, not just promise Valhalla.*

Well, if this analysis is accurate, less than a million voters in key swing states will decide the election. They are the few who will choose.

These are just my thoughts. Those of you who encouraged my Updates are to blame for this long message. If you have any comments, join in. I will forward them to the Political Update network.

## A BITTER BATTLE
## JANUARY 26, 2004

There have been many dirty campaigns and this one will be one of the worst. Both sides are hitting early, often and below the belt. One of the more interesting exchanges is between Bush and Clark. Bush's operatives spread the word that there were ethical and judgmental matters that led to Clark being fired from his last assignment and early retirement from the service. Clark denies this and returning the favor Michael Moore introduced Clark recently with the phrase that this will be a battle "Between the

General and the Deserter." Clark has repeatedly been given the opportunity to disavow Moore's charge of Bush being a deserter and he does not, saying that he has not looked into the matter. Many people think he has made a mistake as desertion is a very serious charge against anyone, especially a President. I don't. Every time someone asks Clark the question it reminds the public about Bush's problems in the National Guard. It's like making the reporters work for Clark. I am sure the President would like to forget the whole discussion and if it is ever brought up in a debate I can't imagine a tougher question for Bush to discuss.

P.S. Tomorrow should continue the excitement of the nomination process it is the publicity and attention the Democrats need to get the public involved. At this point, I just hope the results are close and that Kerry does not run away with the election.

## IT IS KERRY'S RACE TO LOSE.
## WHILE CLARK WAITS IN THE WINGS
## JANUARY 28, 2004

If John Kerry can run effectively in the key swing states, the nomination is his. However if his results are poor or if he backs out of states like South Carolina the Democrats around the country will have to hope that he can win with a "Northern Strategy" by winning ALL the Northern states (which has never been done) or the party will have to turn to one of the other candidates..

Dean is finished, most voters know Edwards' lack of experience stops him from beating Bush and Lieberman should end his pain as soon as possible. The Democrats will need a candidate to appeal to all the categories of voters we covered last week. General Clark is the only one.

Clark can score with the "Anyone but Bush" Group. The Green Party will accept him over Bush, even though Kerry has a good record. The God and Flag crowd love Generals and as far as religion Clark has the best record being Jewish, Protestant and

Catholic in his life. The Lost Battalion Non Voters won't mind that Clark wasn't politically active. And the independents who voted for Bush in 2000 will respect a fellow independent. My cousin Patricia accurately labeled Clark a "Pseudo Democrat" as he has supported Republicans so who better can appeal to the Independents who also vote for both parties. So Clark has a certain appeal to everyone we are after. And remember the main concern of many of these groups is to have a leader that will not sacrifice military strength and national security General Clark is the top candidate for this issue.

On the plus side, the primary in New Hampshire was great with record setting (200,000) participation demonstrating that people are unhappy with Bush and want change. The President knows he is in for a fight and will dump Cheney and Rumsfeld this summer. This will make his ticket stronger no matter who he picks and he has some powerful choices for vice president.

The dogs of politics are now being let loose on Kerry and soon hundreds of millions in advertising will pound his liberalism. Remember they like me are only after the small number of swing voters in the swing states. Kerry will have a tough battle.

On a personal note, I hate to see two aristocrat billionaire family candidates fighting for the White House. Harry Truman, where are you now that we need you.


## THE SADDER BUT WISER VOTERS FOR ME
## JANUARY 31, 2004

Those who haven't had the opportunity to grow old watching the 10 O'clock news can be excused. They just have not lived through the political events that have shaped our history.

McGovern a war hero and great statesman being depicted as weakling, Senator McCain being wiped out by Bush in South Carolina, and last year Max Cleland a man who left three limbs in Vietnam attacked as unpatriotic. The Bush Machine is at their best in this type of dirty fight.

The primaries on Tuesday were exciting, with high voter turnout and the candidates sharpening both their message and delivery. Obviously it is still Kerry's race of lose. We hope that Clark can survive until the big states get a chance to vote. If Kerry wears well and stands up to the opening salvo's from Bush's army i.e. on gay marriages, Teddy Kennedy Clone, etc., it will be his victory.

But if doubts rise as to his ability to beat Bush, the March primaries can change the whole picture. Edwards and Clark fighting each other make it easier for Kerry, but anything can happen. Clark is the toughest candidate against Bush. Stay tuned. The sadder but wiser voters may yet play a role.

## THE GENERAL AND THE DESERTER HAS LEGS
## JANUARY 6, 2004

Last month when we discussed the charge about Bush's service (or lack of service) in the National Guard, we thought it would be an effective issue for Clark in the election. But now it has exploded across the country with numerous articles and faint-hearted responses from the president's campaign.

What we did not understand last month is that four years ago the Clinton legacy of draft avoidance did not allow Gore to raise this issue, but now the war in Iraq plus the record of Kerry and Clark make it a big story. And it is exploding across the country.

But look up some of the articles written this month. The Washington Post has a ton of them. They are powerful and certainly have put Bush on the defensive. Who fights in wars, is an important discussion in our country today.

## LET'S BOW OUR HEAD
## AND THANK HOWARD DEAN
## JANUARY 10, 2004

Those of us who supported any candidate that lost after a long, hard battle know the pain of defeat. Howard Dean is passing into obscurity this week and he certainly deserves our good thoughts. Whether Kerry or Bush wins the election, Dean woke up the electorate and created the excitement that our political system needed and deserved.

It certainly must be painful for Dean. Everyone stole his message once they saw it was working. No doubt they will abandon it in a few months, but without him the election would have been a coronation with 50% of the electorate sitting on their hands.

This is tough week for Dean as he hopes for a miracle in Wisconsin. I certainly did not want him to win but he can rest in peace knowing that he served his country exceptionally well.

## HOW SOON WE FORGET
## FEBRUARY 14, 2004

Three months ago the Democrats were going full speed off a cliff. The "experts" believed that Bush was unbeatable. Gov. Dean had worked hard for two years and seemed to have the nomination wrapped up. The rest were long shots especially John Kerry. Not only were the Democrats going down the tubes but also there was no credible candidate to stand up to the
President and speak the truth. Someone had to rescue the "princess in the tower" and General Clark was drafted to serve his country one more time.

He had a lot going for him. No skeletons in the closet. A brilliant self-made man, fantastic military career, known and respected throughout the world, and one more thing a great wife (big difference from Bush or Kerry).

The primaries were wild and with luck he might have won. But in the final analysis he was an inexperienced politician,
had a poor organization and worst of all just started too late.
The dynamic Iowa caucus was over before he got to the plate.

But his voice was heard. He gave credibility to the attack on the President's policies and had a positive impact on voters throughout the country.

General Clark saw the country's need (not either party but the country); he answered the call and deserves a Medal of Honor and possibly another Purple Heart for the painful battle. We will meet him again.

## THE PRESIDENTIAL CANDIDATES AND OTHER WEALTHY POLITICIANS FEBRUARY 17, 2004

As you might have guessed we are a little discouraged by the fact that two Aristocrat billionaires are probably going to be our choices for President. But, unfortunately, the problem does not stop there.

Next to the Presidency the key political force is the Senate and the vast majority of our Senators are also extremely wealthy... most before they came to office but certainly by the time they leave.

Our Republican Senator spent millions of his own money to win and has tried to do a good job however he is now bored or discouraged and is not running. The leading contender is a Democrat who is spending 20 million of his own money to get the job. Even if they are good, honest people, they are not representative of our country.

To make the point let's turn the pyramid upside down and imagine that the majority of our Senators were from 3rd generation welfare families. They are smart but poor. (By the way they would be more representative of our country than our current Senate). Would you trust their view of the nation? I wouldn't. Obviously for democracy to work we need diversity.

Our Senate is currently working on permanently eliminating the Inheritance Tax. If wealthy families have a few hundred million dollars and can pass it on without any tax how many generations will it take before these elite families have all the money? Congress says they are worried about "the family farm" my guess is that their interests are closer to their "backyard garden."

Our current Inheritance Tax is pretty favorable for the families that are doing well and I am all for paying my share to keep America the land where everyone has a chance to succeed not the home of the privileged few.

A friend recommended an excellent book of this subject, "Wealth and Our Commonwealth Why Americans Should Tax Accumulated Fortunes" by William H. Gates Sr. (Bill's father) and Chuck Collins. It says it all.

## AL SHARPTON SAVES COUNTRY LOT OF TIME AND MONEY FEBRUARY 21, 2004

Other than the congressional investigations of Janet Jackson's breast and the threatened investigation of NCAA Football, the special investigation of our Intelligence agencies are the biggest waste of time. The committee will spend a lot of money, not tell anyone what they found out and in any event will have little impact on our future intelligence operations.

Our intelligence was and is good. We were working with Sadam for many years, had inspectors all over the country, had liaison with other countries that have agents in Iraq, plus hundreds of other intelligence sources. We probably knew what he ate for breakfast every day.

That raises the question. If we weren't after the WMDs, why did we invade Iraq? This is a long subject but let's just say that stability in the Middle East is critical to our security and energy supply. With Saudi Arabia untrustworthy, we needed a new home. Iraq looked like a nice place for our military bases, and Sadam was a no good dictator that we didn't need anymore, so why not.

If you accept this premise you can save you a lot of time. You don't have to read and listen to the discussions about when we are going to leave Iraq, The answer is not for a long, long time.

In the last Debate Al Sharpton was asked about the President misleading the country on why we went to war and if the President knew he was lying. Sharpton responded, "That he hoped the President knew he was lying otherwise we are in much more trouble."

In effect he was right. The President knew why he went to war. Unfortunately he cannot be as direct as we can on the Update. No need for all the money on a yearlong investigation. Our intelligence was good, the President had the facts and now we will have to see how his decision works out.


## THE FIVE LETTER DIRTY WORD
## FEBRUARY 24, 2004

Before the war started the Army estimated that they needed 300,000 troops after the war to maintain order. This figure was attacked by Rumsfeld (as obviously he didn't have that number of troops to send) so the General was fired and a new one gave the estimate the White House wanted. Now we and the Iraqi people are paying the price.

Under International law it is our responsibility as the conquering nation to provide security for the country. It ain't happening. In addition to the Pro Sadam fighters it seems the suicide bombers of the Middle East have hit with devastating effectiveness in the last few weeks they have killed hundreds of Iraqi civilians at this rate we will run out of Iraqi citizens before they run out of suicide candidates. Suicide bombings are tough to stop no matter what we do, but it is a job we are stuck with.

Now the Army is trying to stay out of the cities and stay in armed camps outside the rough areas. This may help keep our casualties down but certainly is not going to convince the UN or other potential supporter that the country is safe for them to get involved.

Our Army is tired. It is tough service. Our critical National Guard and Reserve units are decimated from their extended active duty tours and now are critical to maintaining our position. The army stops any soldier from being discharged but it is at a high cost in moral and impacting new enlistments. We need intelligent, courageous soldiers and the stories from Iraq do not encourage enlistments.

The solution is one of the following:

1. *Pay to get more foreign troops and keep hiring Halliburton to do military support duties. This is very expensive.*

2. *Give up plan to impact other trouble spots in the world. Can't threaten North Korea when we may have to reduce our troops in South Korea to help in the Middle East.*

3. *Use the five letter word that no politician wants to say DRAFT*

My guess is that no matter who wins the election, a draft is in our future. We don't want to give up control of Iraq and certainly can't afford to be a paper tiger during the next five or ten years when we are tied up in Iraq. The draft would be good for the country so that all segments of society will have the investment (sons and daughters) in war, but whether it is good or bad we would like to see at least one candidate face this question honestly and explain how they will solve the military manpower shortage.

They believe we are uninformed or fools and the draft is a five letter dirty word that will not cross their lips… at least until after the election.

## DARTH NADER STRIKES AGAIN
## FEBRUARY 23, 2004

Last month we stated that if Ralph ran he would need bodyguards to attend his own Party meetings. Well Ralph fooled us. He is running as an Independent, not a Green Party Candidate. Not good news for Kerry, but there is some new elements:

1. *His sharp and powerful attacks on the system will continue the excitement of the primaries. It gets people involved and hopefully out to the polls in November. That is good for the country. In addition he may be the new mentor for the Deaniacs and keep them involved in the system. Remember our biggest problem is the millions who don't bother to vote. Nader may help this serious problem.*

2. *After stating how flawed our system is he will attack both parties but this time Bush is the party in power and makes such an easy target that Ralph won't be able to resist.*

3. *Less money and workers will keep Nader off the ballot in many states.*

4. *Ralph wants to keep his movement alive but unless his "balls are bigger than his brains" knows that he will be "persona non grata" if he is the deciding force in the election. Our guess is that after he has delivered his message he will tone back the campaign and let the voters choose between Bush and Kerry.*

5. *Finally it comes down to the voters on Election Day. Do the Naderites vote for a cause or a potential president? My guess is that this time most will vote with their brain, not their hearts. And Kerry will get 70% of those votes.*

## ISN'T POLITICS FUN? TIME TO BRING THE MONROE DOCTRINE UP TO DATE OR GET SOME NEW GUNBOATS
## MARCH 4, 2004

It was very sad watching Secretary Powell and Vice President Cheney trying to keep a straight face when caught lying about their role in overthrowing the president of Haiti. How could they imagine the CIA would be so incompetent, but the problem is they are using 1950 ideas that do not work in this world of fast communications?

First we need to revise the Monroe Doctrine (been done many times) and say we only want governments in the Western Hemisphere that support the U.S. If they do we will help them a little and if not we will throw them out. If we stated that clearly President Aristide would have gone along because the murderers that would replace him with would be much worse for the people of that sad nation.

If not the Administration should at least figure out how to change governments with some modern tools. Back in the 50's we could overthrow a government (like Guatemala) and no one knew about it for four or five years and by that time no one cared. Some of our revolutions like Chile got a little more notice but since we were throwing out a Socialist, many of us thought it was a good idea.

Unfortunately for Bush and Powell, there are too many independent reporters all over the world and too many people have cell phones and watch developments as they happen on CNN. Our military coups are just outdated.

If nothing else, having to lie on world television is not good for the Vice President's heart so we better keep him in his bunker or get up to date on our revolutionary techniques.

## THE BONFIRE OF GREED IS BURNING
## MARCH 6, 2004

The last twenty years were filled with executives who professed their right to be the new imperial aristocracy. They were clearly described in fiction and movies. Who can forget Sherman McCoy in the Bonfire of the Vanities who thought it unfair that he had to struggle to live on a salary of million dollars a year or Gordon Gekko who established that "Greed is Good" in the movie Wall Street.

This is a truly an American phenomenon. European business people in similar positions have a totally different view of their value to their companies. When we were visiting another country they questioned us on why they are so selfish. It is tough question to answer. The ratio of salary of top executives to the workers in their company is staggering and may be burning up the faith of many upper and lower management workers.

Take for example the President of Cendant Corporation. His 2003 salary and bonus was 23 million, not including stock options! Sure he may have done a great job but so did a lot of people at the other end of the organizational chart. Is any one person worth that much? What is their responsibility to society and to give stockholders and employees a chance to climb the ladder?

Excessive salaries and crooks like Enron have seriously damaged the faith our citizens have in capitalism. Probably why Martha got zapped. The Jury wanted to fight back against this privileged class. She did very little wrong compared to most corporate greed cases but don't expect any Jury to have mercy in this climate.

## THE LULL BEFORE THE STORM
## MARCH 8, 2004

Several Updaters have asked why we have not written about the election in the past weeks. Well basically nothing is happening. The race was decided a month ago and the primaries only gave Democrats a way to get free advertising and Edwards a chance to continue his drive for the Vice Presidency. But we do not minimize the importance of the election.

## BILL CLINTON IS BEGINNING
## TO LOOK GOOD TO REPUBLICANS
## MARCH 12, 2004

Sort of funny how time changes perceptions. The man Republicans loved to hate is now being cited as an example of an honest and effective President. Gone are the jokes about "is" and "Monica" as one investigation after other piles on Bush about why we went to war, who is profiting from it, etc. Now Republicans point to the high level of professionalism in Clinton's presidential campaigns (compared to Kerry and Bush) and of course they are touting his free trade policies and longing for a return to his budget management. It is truly amazing.

## THE "HILL" IS ALIVE
## WITH THE SOUND OF MONEY
## MARCH 9, 2004

Two weeks ago we had the pleasure of being a lobbyist for food programs and nutrition education. Through the experience we learned the power of lobbying and petitioning your congress. They do listen to their constituents but it is a complicated process and certainly financial "support" is helpful.

This brings back a question we have had in the past. Is it better to have a Congressman or Senator that is extremely wealthy before they go to Congress or one of more average wealth? Which one will be more immune to big money contributors?

In Illinois two Republican candidates for Senate are very wealthy and we wrote about the Democrat who has spent over 30 million of his own money on the race. Maybe our founding fathers meant for the Senate to be for the aristocracy and the Congress for more common folks.

It is an interesting question and Tuesday we will find out who wins in Illinois. In any event it seems that if they aren't wealthy before they get to Washington most are by the time they leave the "Hill" is definitely alive with money one way or another.


## THE PAIN IN SPAIN FALLS
## MAINLY ON OUR PLAINS
## MARCH 15, 2004

The bombing in Spain and the subsequent reaction of the Spanish voters to change leadership is a watershed event that will affect our future. Al Queda has once again been more successful than anyone could have imagined. Their timing and deadly attack will make it much more difficult for our government to get support without total UN control. It is a tough situation for our President and the probability of attacks in our country to influence our election is certainly increased. It is a pain for Spain and the entire world.

## MY OH MY OBAMA
## MARCH 17, 2004

Jack Ryan, one of the three multi-millionaires in the Republican Senate primary won. Jack is an attractive candidate with a Harvard Law Degree but has never been in politics.

The surprising news is that Obama easily won the Democrat primary. He defeated everyone from the machine candidate to the novice that spent 40 million and got only 10% of the vote. Obama is also a Harvard Law Grad but has been active in state politics while teaching at the University of Chicago Law School. He is getting immediate national attention. Watch for him. He is a fast rising star.

These two young men mirror their Presidential candidates on most issues so it will be a meaningful campaign.


## TWO TOUGH CHOICES
## FOR VICE PRESIDENT
## MARCH 18, 2004

Normally Kerry would select a Vice President who could bring him one or two states, but this year he has a greater need. He is in good position on most issues such as the economy and deficits, but needs to counter the "War President" by bolstering his image on defending our country against terrorism.

 Our choice again would be General Wesley Clark (no groans please). Bush and Cheney aren't going to talk about being patriots or the importance of military power if they are facing Kerry and Clark.

In addition, Clark is not a traditional Democrat who might appeal to the independent swing voter.

---

Since there are many new Updaters we are attaching our original analysis (of January 25th) on why Clark would have made the strongest presidential candidate. It didn't turn out the way we thought but most of the thinking on how Clark could win the votes of "The Few Who Will Choose" is still valid.

Well that solves Kerry's problem, now what about the President's VP. Cheney doesn't bring him any votes and will cost him a lot of independent voters who are upset about Halliburton being investigated for a billion in over charges. Why not make a change. He has many excellent candidates to pick from such as Mayor Rudolph Guliani or Senator Elizabeth Dole - both would also bring his platform toward the center, which is where his campaign is headed.

Obviously Bush is a loyal man and needs Cheney's advice, but it would be much better for the President if his Doctors would check out Dick's heart again.

## YESTERDAY'S AGENT ORANGE
## AND TODAY'S ELECTION CAMPAIGN
## MARCH 21, 2004

Viet Nam is like a bad dream that keeps coming back Dow Chemical made Agent Orange, a particular deadly herbicide. They knew it would affect everything it touched, but kept making it and the Pentagon used it in unnecessary high concentrations to defoliate the jungle and kill crops. It has left a legacy of death and disease for future generations in Viet Nam and to a lesser extent to our Veterans. Many have died including Senator Kerry's closest friend in the military. And of course Kerry has had his cancerous prostate removed.

After many years Dow paid 180 million to settle lawsuits (it's a good thing Dow wasn't serving extra hot coffee at McDonalds) and the Veterans Administration set up an entire program. Thousands of Veterans are now being treated from the effects of Agent Orange.

This issue will come up in the election. First questions will be raised about Kerry's health. This is a legitimate question and may hurt him. But when that issue is discussed it will follow that Kerry fought the government for years about Agent Orange and helped get our Veterans the care they deserved.

And once again, Viet Nam will be debated.

It is not Bush's fault that he avoided Viet Nam and this type of risk. Tens of thousands did or would have done the same if they had the clout. But the fact that Kerry lives with this long-term effect makes his decisions on the current war more credible.

To put it bluntly, it is easy to be tough when someone else and someone else's family live with the pain from the fight.

P.S. We fear a similar scenario is being played out from the first Gulf War and now possibly in Iraq. Will our veterans be paying the price for the rest of their lives not knowing why they are sick? We tend to focus on the 500 who have been killed in Iraq. But more painful are the thousands who are wounded or develop long-term physical and mental diseases. Unfortunately, the effects of war go on long after the shooting stops.

# The War

## THE TRANSITION GOVERNMENT IS READY AND RARING TO GO MARCH 30, 2004

There is a lot of talk and concern as to how we are going to turn Iraq back to the Iraqis on June 30. Some say the Bush Team is not prepared. It seems to us that this is one area that has been well planned.

Long before 9/11 the Bush administration was working with Ahmed Chalabi and his group of exiles. They provided the bogus info on WMD and all sorts of stories designed to get them back to Iraq. We financed him and his personal army. They were brought to Iraq before the war started even though he was discredited throughout the Middle East and under Indictment for robbing his own bank corporation. But no matter how much he lied or how bad his information we loved him and paid hundreds of thousands a month. And he brought along all his friends. The day after the war ended a few of his friends formed a new corporation to start raking in the money with contracts on everything including arming the new Iraq Army. Our country is paying them hundreds of millions of dollars... talk about outsourcing.

Chalabi is on the governing council and no doubt he will be in charge on July 1. The Iraqis have no faith in him and if you heard him on any interview you wouldn't either. But he will be taking care of our money and working with us on oil, future involvement of our long term military bases. Chalabi will leave the religious issue alone it just doesn't generate much profit.

It is obvious we need a friendly government in Iraq if not why invade. But can't Washington come up with someone a little less odious.

## HERE'S A SCARY THOUGHT
## APRIL 3, 2004

What if the President and his key advisors felt they wanted to go to war to remove a Terrible Dictator? The President knew his people were against war because they had lived through a bitter one in the past, but he had to move fast four years in office passes very quickly.

Well his team figured it out. If they could get a third party to attack us the people would be "mad as hell" and he could go to war against the third party and of course the Terrible Dictator. This was tough. First they had to get the third party fighting mad at us and then give them a great target.

And it worked. The third party attacked and everyone rushed to defend our country. The President was hailed as a hero in defending our country.

Of course, there was a problem. Some people suspected what happened and established a Commission to get the facts. Well you couldn't expect the President's advisors to be anxious to testify and as usual most people soon forgot about how the whole thing started.

Well actually this was more than a scary thought. It was history. The President was Roosevelt. The Dictator was Hitler. The third party was Japan and of course we all "Remember Pearl Harbor" and the Pearl Harbor Commission.

Oh did you think we were talking about President Bush, Sadam Hussein, Al Queda, and 9/11. SHAME ON YOU!

But wait a minute maybe you do have something there. Oh well, either way we thought you might like this little review of history.

## NO WAY OUT NO WAY OUT!
## APRIL 6, 2004

In the second act of the Broadway hit show "The Producers", the conspirators (Max and Leo) are caught when the play they designed to fail becomes a gigantic hit. Max starts a mournful cry "No way out, no way out no way out."

The situation in Iraq is beginning to make us moan the same refrain.

- *We need to win the people over to our side but our soldiers cannot fight people one day and make friends with them the next.*

- *We wanted to avoid a religious war but it seems right around the corner.*

- *We need more troops and will have to extend enlistments and tours of duty. Tough days for our soldiers.*

- *We can pretend to turn over the government on June 30, but the Iraqis and the world will view it as a sad joke.*

- *We can't leave Iraq without making the Middle East a mess for decades and losing what's left of our prestige.*

- *We can't get the UN to rescue us (unless we give them all the fruits of controlling Iraq) because that would be like asking someone to trade places when you are in a hurricane and they are relaxing at home.*

If anyone has a plan, now is the time to produce. If not we can only hope and pray for a solution to appear before the final curtain.

Right now we think Max had it just about exactly right.


## WHERE IS BILL WHEN GEORGE REALLY NEEDS HIM?
## APRIL 11, 2004

They both went to Yale, but evidently George cut his English classes and now could use some help. And when it comes to using the English language to hide what you are saying Bill is the master.

Every statement about 9/11 goes something like, "If we knew that they were going to attack New York and Washington on Sept. 11, we would have taken strong immediate action." Or a hundred sentences that use words like "no current" "no documented" or "no specific information" All this double talk makes their statement accurate but are designed to hide the facts. The truth is easy to say. But you have to be clever to mislead without lying.

Clinton's statements about his relationship with Monica, didn't work for him but it took a few days to interpret what he said. With the Bush team it is just too obvious. Certainly they did not have specific information about the attack, but it looks like dozens of government officials had a good idea what could happen and were not surprised when it did.

If George would ask Bill for a little help, he might get it after all no one wants to see our leaders flunk English.

## WHAT WAS THAT ALL ABOUT?
## APRIL 13, 2004

When the President scheduled the Prime Time Press Conference we were sure he had good news to report, a clearer explanation of why we invaded Iraq or how the new government will be organized for July 1. Nothing no news, no explanations, no new plan not even a small apology.

It is true that the President needs to be seen as personally directing the nation, but why today after two weeks of setbacks in Iraq and embarrassing information coming out of the 9/11 Commission?

President Bush was ill prepared for the aggressive questioning. He failed to answer the most direct questions including ones that could have been answered strongly. He stalled and rambled repeated himself over and over went back to sound bites, etc. It will be interesting to see what positive comments anyone can find to say about this evening. Maybe his spinners will just attack the reporters for their negative questions.

Sometimes you can look for a complicated explanation when the answer is simple. Our guess is that his advisors made a big mistake. This was not the day for Prime Time George.

## BOOKS 4: BUSH 0
## APRIL 18, 2004

It's a good thing the President is running against Kerry instead of the books about his administration. So far the books have been devastating, and the Woodward one seems to be the most damaging mainly because Bush made the mistake of being personally interviewed by the toughest and smartest reporter. His advisors seem to have made one poor decision after another and in the future they will probably keep the President totally under wraps.

Without these books, Bush would be leading Kerry by double digits. Kerry has a difficult position on the war, but more about that in the next Update.


## AND NOW LADIES AND GENTLEMEN THE INCREDIBLE BALANCING ACT OF JOHN KERRY ON THE HIGH WIRE!
## APRIL 21, 2004

Howard Dean was the straight talking politician who said it the way he saw it i.e. Bush created the war in Iraq and if elected he would end it as quickly as possible. Kerry saw how popular this position was so he delivered the same message and won the nomination. But, the election is a much more complicated matter.

Bush is the President and he has put our country's cards on the table. We can't change direction every time we have another President "oops sorry we invaded you Iraq, but we have to run now see you later." If Kerry campaigns on pulling out of Iraq it would cause confusion and damage to our country's position. So Kerry being an intelligent politician and patriotic American has to support the basic Bush policy and make his criticism very obtuse.

So the question is with this muted position, can he win? Here are three groups that will be watching the Senator carefully he needs to convince all of them.

First Kerry has to hold his Democratic base that believes we are in a dangerous unjust war. And who can argue when the administration's key response to 711 is to plan the invasion of Iraq with Saudi Arabia (when no Iraqis were involved in 711 but all the money and most of the terrorists came from Saudi Arabia), These Democrats believe we are in this terrible situation due to the incompetence of the Bush and want their candidate to shout it loud and clear.

Next a key group the "few who will choose" independent voters. They understand the problem of changing policy in the middle of a war. Kerry's antiwar activity after service in Viet Nam adds to their concern as to how he could handle this mess. They know Bush is off in the wild blue yonder but may believe changing horses is too dangerous.

Finally the Deaniacs and new voters that are violently anti-war and who may not vote at all if they don't see a big difference between Kerry and Bush. Out of spite they may turn to another candidate, our "old friend" Ralph Nader. He never worries about the effect of what he says and if he attracts more voters than his current 6 percent, Bush should consider himself lucky he jumped into a barrel of manure and came out smelling like a rose.

Well, there is a long way to go and this will be an events driven election, but.

Kerry is on the high wire and he better have a safety net.

## LISTEN CAREFULLY AND YOU WILL HEAR THE CALL FROM IRAQ." GET US OUT!" MAY 2, 2004

The Generals are finally getting enough courage to speak out. They put their stars ahead of their troops when they followed Rumsfeld's war plans and ignored their own experts. They have no plan to win and no way to get out. They can't attack in force without losing International Support. They can't fight in the streets without heavy loses that Washington does not want. Poorly lead soldiers like the Prison Guards will bring one public relations disaster after another and the public will gradually lose faith in their mission. The extent of their desperation was obvious as they now turn to Sadam's Army for help.

These Generals have been here before in Viet Nam. They know how politics and Washington works. If Bush is reelected he will stay in his cocoon and let the carnage continue and if Kerry is elected he will spend two years trying to declare victory and leave. Either way the military will be left holding the bag and our nation will be weakened in the eyes of friends and foes.

Obviously the Generals cannot hold a briefing and say we lost the war. Instead they are sending a call to their retired comrades in Washington to get them out before Iraq becomes Viet Nam. Nobody wants it happen again.

Our soldiers and our country deserve much more.


## VIET NAM DOES NOT LET US REST
## MAY 4, 2004

Every event in Iraq plays out in relation to our history in Viet Nam. It is hard to ignore the parallels.

One of the turning points in losing the war in Viet Nam was the massacre of 500 civilians in the village of My Lai. It turned public opinion against the war. The army focused on Lt. Calley who is still serving a life sentence at hard labor. But who encouraged and made his action possible. The Generals washed their hands and did not take the blame that was rightfully theirs. They wanted body counts and they wanted to pacify the opposition.

This time it looks again like a few junior officers and poorly trained National Guard soldiers will take the fall. And the people who are really responsible will go home pretending that they are heroes. Who failed to supervise these soldiers? Who put the so-called "contractors" in charge of interrogating prisoners? By what law will these civilian contractors be tried or will they just take their $1,000 a day pay and go home? The people in Washington who put them in charge are responsible for this moral and public relations disaster.

This time let's go beyond the photos and get to the guilty party.

## RUMSFELD THE REALIST
## MAY 7, 2004

The sound you heard in Washington today was Rumsfeld falling on his sword to save the president. His only concern is not being named as a war criminal by some international organization. Resignation is on the way after all the bad news is out. Truly a sad day for our country and especially for our military forces.

## A THREE-ACT PLAY:
## PRINCE COLIN OF WASHINGTON

As we await Act Three of this exciting play let's review Act One and Two:

### Act One

*The Pride of the Kingdom*

Prince Colin is the pride of the crown and respected throughout the land. He is a mighty warrior that led a victorious army in distant lands. Other Kingdoms also admire him as a man of peace. The King loves him and considers making him the next King. Prince Colin can do no wrong, but says he and the princess would prefer to serve the crown rather than rule it is too difficult a life.

## Act Two (ten years later)

*Now the Fool*

The King has passed the throne to his rather slow son. Prince Colin tries to help the new King, but there is much intrigue in the castle and diabolical members of the court want to control the King they scheme and plot the demise of Prince Colin. Soon he is ridiculed throughout the land and ignored by other Kingdoms. The Prince is despondent and even fearful for his life the long knives are out.

Should he join the old king in exile, or put on his sword and fight his enemies. The act ends as he recites the famous line "To Be Myself or Not To Be Myself."

## Act Three (one year later)

*Time to Decide*

Now the audience is on edge. Will Prince Colin fight like the warrior he is and destroy the palace guard? Will he run from the fight as a coward? Will he sacrifice his life for the King? The suspense is unbearable as the curtain rises on Act Three.


# FROM HERO TO SCAPEGOAT
# IN ONE EASY LESSON
# MAY 11, 2004

Last month our government was lauding the National Guard for the tremendous job they have done at extreme personal cost. Being away from their home and jobs for repeated calls to active duty all because Rumsfeld had this convoluted idea that we don't have to have a big regular Army to fight a war.

Well their claim to fame was deserved but didn't last long enough for them to even get home to a hero's welcome. The hearing today showed that many of them will be the scapegoat and their future destroyed.

No one wants to be associated with war crimes, but this session today was brutal. When Rumsfeld and his Pentagon team saw the danger to their careers they circled the wagons and threw the National Guard out.

The claim of the soldiers that they were only following orders will be a sure loser, but it is another silly decision by Rumsfeld. Anyone who spent even one month in the Army will not believe that the National Guard General and her troops initiated these abuses. The responsibility clearly goes to Rumsfeld and General Meyer.

Now we wonder how many senior officers are going to come to their defense of these enlisted men? What will Prince Colin say? And of course the real decision makers, what will we say?

This situation may tell us more about ourselves than our leaders.

## NEW CAMPAIGN PLAN FOR JOHN: LET BUSH RUN AGAINST BUSH
## MAY 14, 2004

Several Updaters have written that Kerry should take a position against the war, but his plan is to be all things to all people so that he can be the "other candidate" that will win by default.

It seems that no matter how many mistakes the President makes the election will still be decided by the "few who will choose" a small percentage of voters in 8 or 10 swing states. So far Kerry is not only not gaining votes, but is actually helping the President. He is taking the focus away from the terrible situation that the country is in and away from the real decision the referendum on the Presidency of George Bush.

Kerry would be better off going skiing. If the few who will choose are happy with the President he will be reelected and if not he will lose.

This new campaign would have other benefits. No money needed for campaigning, less stress for his staff and no silly meetings with supporters who have already made up their mind. Let everyone focus on what Bush says and does as he flies around the country.

In the battle between Bush and Bush, Kerry has an excellent chance to win. The only thing he should focus on is selecting the best Vice President to help him lead the country if he is elected.

We know Kerry won't take this advice, but if he did, the next six months would be quieter and more interesting.

## THE WAR COMES TO WASHINGTON OR HOW THE ACCUSERS BECAME THE ACCUSED IN 72 HOURS MAY 16, 2004

As we reported earlier some Generals lost faith in Rumsfeld and his war plan. Now it seems to us that they are leaking classified information on the Prison abuse story as a way to force a change in policy. The amount of secret details that are being disclosed about the Bush/Rumsfeld/Ashcroft policy on Detainees is amazing. Certainly the President did not expect his own Army, CIA and State Department to turn him in, but that seems to be the case. They are bringing the War to Washington.

Violations of the Geneva Conventions happen in all wars, but it seems that we developed formalized orders and plans that fly right in the face of this International agreement. We can't imagine any government leaving such a clear paper trail to their door. We expected this scenario to develop over several months, but this change happened in only a few days.

So where 72 hours ago the Pentagon was going to sacrifice a National Guard General or Colonel and 10 or so MPs, now the Pentagon leaders are in a fight for their own survival. They don't have anyone to throw to the wolves but themselves.

## NOW RUMMY IS REALLY IN TROUBLE
## MAY 18, 2004

For the past year Rumsfeld has been accused of everything from tricking the President into war to torturing the detainees in Iraq, but now he is really is trouble. The financial powers have been whispering for the past month that his policies are destroying the economy and today they came right out and said it "This Is the Rumsfeld Market!"

Well you can imagine the concern at the Defense Department and at the White House. A guy can make a lot of mistakes but you better not kill a rally on Wall Street. Now we will see if lower stock prices have more impact than higher casualties.

Oh well, we bet this is one of those days that Donald wishes he was back in Illinois.

## NOW IT'S BOOKS 5 AND BUSH 0
## MAY 23, 2004

This was another tough week for the President. A new book by General Zinni accuses the President of listening only to the neo-cons and letting them make every possible mistake. Lot of implications for the entire Middle East that no doubt we will be discussing in the next weeks. But It is a prime example of the "Generals Attack on Washington" that we reported on May 2 they are out to get the President and his team.

 In the meantime the Democrats are raising the stakes. Congressional Leader Nancy Pelosi says the President has no clothes that he is simply incompetent under the control of the White House cabal tough language but again targeting the key advisors around the President.

But with all this help Kerry doesn't make much headway. He needs a new campaign manager. Two days ago Kerry's camp proposed the ridiculous idea of not accepting the nomination at the convention so they could bypass the law on spending. I guess they still don't understand that they are after the "few who will choose" and by avoiding an election law that thinking people wanted for many years is not the way to win their vote. The law may not be fair and it may not be right, but it is the law. This tricky maneuver would bring a lot of ridicule when their goal should be to keep Bush running against himself. His talk to the Republican congressional team was a disaster. This week he is going to start explaining the war to all of us. If (and that is as big if) the Kerry Campaign is smart they will keep their mouth shut and the spotlight on the President.

Bike riding in Texas is tough but the President is good at it. He is, however, going to have to be more careful on those dangerous Washington trails.

## MEMORIAL DAY 2004
## MAY 31, 2004

This Memorial Day received new emphasis with the dedication of the WWII Memorial. There has been an enormous amount of publicity; heart felt stories and historical programs about other wars. Memorial Day has always been an important time to pay our respects to Veterans but doing right by them is much more than a day filled with parades, flags and speeches. The new Memorial is an example of how good things can go wrong. Let's review a little history.

WWII was a national effort. We all had family, friends and neighbors who served, saw Gold Stars go up in windows and every man, woman and child tried to contribute to the war effort. This contrasts with today when few of us know those who are fighting and the country thinks it is unusual when a successful football player wants to serve his country.

The 16 million veterans of WWII did their duty. You rarely heard any of them talk or complain about their sacrifice or the horrors of war. They did their job and service to their country. In their hearts they silently remembered their lost comrades not once a year, but every day. Most important they were welcomed home by our entire country.

The same thing happened to a lesser extent in the Korean "Conflict" the veterans returned home and tried to put their life back together. Many served in both WWII and Korea. It was difficult but they were welcomed home by their country.

The change started in Vietnam. Once again our military fought courageously but the war was unpopular and they returned home to a country that was divided and a public that ignored them or worse. They were not welcomed home and only years later did they organize their own sad parades across America. Thousands never rejoined society.

As the years passed, the country realized they had to make up for this terrible insult so we built the Vietnam Memorial.

Well then a few misguided congressmen thought we needed a memorial to the veterans of the Korean Conflict and the small but dramatic memorial was built. Then following the chain, discussion started on the WWII Memorial and twenty years later we have it. Can a memorial for the Veterans of WWI be far behind? The first Gulf War the current Iraq War will probably take their place in line.

Congress has seen the danger and is no longer funding these memorials but the fact is they are not needed. Even worse they may end up like the new one being an ineffective tribute to the four hundred thousand who died and the hundreds of thousands who lived with their wounds and disabilities. In any event they don't need art, marble and concrete to remember their war the playing of Taps says it all. It is up to the rest of us to educate our children about our history and what "service to your country" means.

Memorials are not important. What is important is to respect our veterans with deeds. It is how we take care of the veterans who never made it out of the hospitals, how their widows and children are treated and most important how we respect the new veterans coming back from Iraq.

Our current soldiers may end up like the Viet Nam Veterans. This we cannot allow to happen. They did not declare war, we did. We didn't serve, they did.

## IT'S TIME TO GET OUT THE WHITE HOUSE OUIJA BOARD JUNE 3, 2004

The President like Kerry might be better off if he just stays out of sight. Not much to talk about.

Quite a day. George Tenet goes down fighting. The White House was starting to get rid of baggage (like General Sanchez) and the CIA decided not to way for Cheney's axe fall when they are blamed for 9/11 and the lack of WMD in Iraq. Last week Tenet wiped out Chalibi (Cheney's pick to run Iraq), put their CIA Iraqi in charge and today resigned. The President may have been the only one in Washington who was surprised.

Other battles between the branches of our government are out in the open. The CIA and the Military are attacking the Pentagon. Rumsfeld has lost power and it is a good thing he is not reading the papers or he might find out that he also is resigning for family reasons. Ashcroft and Tom Ridge keep fighting over who is in charge of putting the country on alert. The Vice President is sending the State Department out to be embarrassed again and the Republicans are starting to jump ship by stockpiling sound bites for future use on "how they advised the President to change policy in Iraq and control spending."

And the President wonders who he can trust and is getting out his Ouija Board to fill future appointments. This is not fun.

## TIME TO ISSUE NEW SIDE ARMS: DIGITAL CAMERAS
## JUNE 5, 2004

We all know the facts about the prisoner abuse. It has been reported by leading newspapers even those like the Wall Street Journal that are supporting the President. To sum it up in a few sentences:

After 9/11 the President said that Al Qaeda prisoners would not be covered by the Geneva Conventions and in effect would disappear from the national and international legal system.(The Supreme Court has yet to review this decision.) Then the President inferred to the American Public (and more importantly to our soldiers) that Iraq was involved in the attack on 9/11, Of course the President now says that Iraq had nothing to do with 9/11 and that Iraqi prisoners would be treated in accordance with the Geneva Conventions, but it was tough for the military and a lot of our citizens to keep the difference between Al Qaeda and Iraqis clear. Then the hunt for WMD's became desperate and the peace went sour so the Secretary of Defense made up a phony ruling and said let's get the prisoners to talk. He sent some "special contractors" to show military intelligence how to get the job done. The CIA wisely ran in the other direction

Hundreds of people know these facts, so why deny it. Either way the pain is going up the chain with General Sanchez being only the first. The Pentagon hopes the American Public will get tired of the stories and tune out the problem because it is too painful and it is terrible to even think about viewing a thousand photos and videos of prisoner abuse. But the story won't go away in an election year and with world opinion from the Pope on down condemning the abuse. Telling the truth and saying you are sorry is the only intelligent action. Every Court Martial of National Guard officers and enlisted personnel will only make the matter worse.

Plus if everyone knows the facts why waste money on the congressional investigation.The Committee is getting nowhere. They cannot even get a honest copy of the Taguba Report (The Pentagon left out 2000 pages when they last gave Congress the "complete" report) and the witnesses seem to have no problem fabricating stories that go back to the "Hear No Evil, See No Evil, You Can't Blame Me for Evil" defense.

 P. S. On the humorous side, If you want to put a stop to these abuses let's give soldiers a new side arm digital cameras. Photos seem to be the best defense for low ranking officers and enlisted personnel that are going to prison. After all you can't send a private to prison for doing something wrong if he has a photo of General standing next to him.


## TALK ABOUT HAVING A BAD LAWYER!
## JUNE 10, 2004

The President's lawyers made a mistake that will haunt Bush for the rest of his Presidency and probably his life. They not only did not protect the President but also used him to save the Pentagon, civilian firms and of course the top Generals that can now say they were only following orders. It won't work but it gives them some cover. (We all remember what happened to the Germans at Nuremberg who used this defense). This time the lawyers built a paper trail of authorizing torture right to the President's desk.

Contrast this with President Reagan in his biggest legal challenge. Congress wanted to impeach him over the Iran Contra deal, which was in violation of our country's policy of not negotiating with kidnappers and hostage takers. Reagan's lawyers protected the President so well that he probably had no idea what was going on. There certainly was no written trail signed by Reagan to trade Arms for Hostages.

Rumsfeld is cooked anyway but the Bush memo was designed to give cover to the dozens of misguided officials who broke crucial International Agreements and U.S. Policy without any understanding of how they were affecting our country and specifically our soldiers in Iraq and in future conflicts. We imagine Bush is violent over this stupidity and we hope is looking for a new lawyer.

## ARE THEY IN DENIAL?
## JUNE 15, 2004

Well it is time to get back to the campaign and an interesting one it is. One of the amazing aspects is that neither party is proud or excited about their candidate but both seem supremely confident that they are going to win. Their mutual reasoning seems to be that they under estimate their opponent so much that they do not see how they can lose. Republicans totally disrespect Kerry and Democrats can't imagine that anyone would want to reelect George Bush.

As stated before, we believe the choice of VP for both parties will be crucial. Bush is cleaning house and would be much stronger without Cheney. And it is crunch time for Kerry. He would have been better off naming his VP last month, but now probably has to wait for the convention. It at least will give people a reason to tune in other than to hear Hillary and Bill.

We still believe General Clark would have been the best Presidential candidate and is now Kerry's strongest VP. Remember the parties are focused on the "few who will choose" and those voters will decide on the economy and national security. The economy is in trouble but now is out of the control of the candidates and into the hands of Alan Greenspan. National security is critical and if there is another attack in our country will be the deciding factor. Which candidate knows how to best defend the country will be the question and on this matter General Clark would be a big plus for Kerry.

In the meantime, we hope Kerry and Bush can get their act together. So far they have spent tons of money and haven't gained an inch with the critical few who will choose. Both parties need new thinking, clear ideas and good communication.

We deserve it.

## LIKE WINNING THE LOTTERY
## JUNE 20, 2004

To most of us a war means defending our country, a necessary evil or a tragedy for all involved. But that is not the way everyone feels about it. Instead many look forward to war as a chance to win the lottery or get another star on their shoulder. This has been true in all of our wars but unfortunately Iraq looks like the "big tuna" of profiteering. For example, today's headline in the Chicago Tribune was:

"Insiders Shape Postwar Iraq Republican Ties Often Trumped Experience in Coalition."

It is an in-depth story about how power in Iraq is going to the political friends of the administration instead of State Department and other experts. It reported about a Stuart Bowen Jr. who just went from being a lobbyist getting 30 million in Iraqi contracts for his company to Inspector General for the Coalition Provisional Authority his duty (you guessed it) watching out for corruption. (Take your choice laugh or cry.)

---

Every war in our country's history has had their share of profiteers and they certainly come from all political parties. Fortunes are made and power achieved quickly. When war is on the horizon they line up not for the draft but for the graft. This goes from top to bottom those that want to steal a billion or so on a contract to those that want to overcharge a soldier's family for a place to live when housing is short.

In President Eisenhower's famous farewell address he warned us to watch out for the military industrial complex that impacts our economic, political and spiritual lives. He said the potential for the disastrous rise of misplaced power exists and will exist. And one of Arthur Miller's most powerful plays, All My Sons, shows the danger and impact of war profiteering. It is an old, sad story.

Profiteering is not a subject we like to think about, but since it has such an impact on whether or not we succeed in Iraq and the war on terror, it cannot be ignored.


## MONICA, BILL AND YOU
## JUNE 24, 2004

Historians normally do not evaluate a presidency for decades, but Bill Clinton has started the process with his memoirs. One painful element that will get a lot of attention is the impact of Monica on 9/11. The question is: How could Clinton focus on being President when he was under constant vicious attack.

Clinton says being hounded by political enemies and being impeached did not stop him from competently running the defense of the country. He has a big psychological explanation that is ridiculous. It is impossible for any President to focus on these massive challenges when your presidency (and to a lesser extent your marriage) is on the line.

Even more important the FBI was spending 20 times the effort chasing Bill as they were Osama's operatives in the U.S. Clinton says he would have fired the Director for incompetence except that the political climate did not allow him to take this action. Congress and every part of our government focused on Whitewater and Monica when they all knew dangerous terrorists were challenging us.

The 9/11 Commission should ask Ken Starr what emotional shape the President was in as he chased him from one old girl friend to another. However, don't look for the Congress to investigate this important prelude to 9/11 as they led the charge and bear the real responsibility. They will gladly agree with Clinton's explanation.

We write this Update not to castigate Clinton or the fools who destroyed him, but rather as a lesson. The current climate of hate must be toned down or Bush will, like Clinton, soon be operating at half his "usual speed" because he will be worried about impeachment, war crimes, ridicule, history, etc. Under this pressure he may have made or will make similar blunders.

If you think Bush is a disaster vote for Kerry. But remember that now he is making life or death decisions regarding your children. Monica's "sexual favors" cost our country a high price. Learn from the stupidity of the Clinton haters who destroyed Clinton and possibly our nation's future.

Don't repeat the mistake with Bush.

# HOLD ON TO YOUR HATS
# THREE DAYS AND COUNTING
# JUNE 27, 2004

It is pretty easy to see what we would "like" to happen with the new Iraqi government.

1. *Iraqis make the decisions but we have the final word.*

2. *The bombings and attacks slow down as our enemy sees the battle is futile and life improves for the average Iraqi.*

3. *The Iraqi police control the streets and our soldiers stay in fortified positions building permanent bases.*

4. *We control the oil and protect the pipelines.*

5. *We work hard and spend hard to make things better for the Iraqis.*

6. *We try to have a "real" election, but if it doesn't work, they have will have to work it out for themselves.*

This type of control has been tried many times. Currently, we see it is not working in Afghanistan, but is has worked in the past. For example in the last century the British controlled Iraq for 30 years before it fell apart and we ended up with rulers like Sadam.

In any event let's not delude ourselves. We know what we want to happen but the rest is hope and prayers.

# FAHRENHEIT 9/11 IS A PHENOMENON
# JUNE 29, 2004

There was so much talk about Michael Moore's movie that we thought it would go down just as the talking heads on television said the Bush lovers would not go {working on the see no evil theory} and the Bush haters would relish every minute resulting in very little impact on the election.

Everyone may have been wrong. Many people found it irresistible to go to the movie and were amazed by the content. Actually there was little new in the film but to some it seems to have been very informative. For example at the showing we went to you could have heard a pin drop when they showed wounded veterans evidently a shock to some in attendance.

Updater Cousin Ron (who viewed the film from a professional view as well as political) sent us this comment:

"The film may have a few flaws but the overall picture is one terrific documentary. You probably heard about the scene when Bush reads to schoolchildren while the planes crash into the World Trade Center. He continues to read after being told of the tragedy. His indecision and inaction are startling. It's worth seeing the film just for that bit of editing."

It seems that the initial White House attack had the opposite effect and attracted many people to see the movie. I guess what someone says you shouldn't see is what you want to see, so the distribution is growing in all areas, both red and blue.

We doubt if the administration will challenge any facts in the movie since almost all are a matter of public record and bringing out one or two minor errors would just validate the other charges and give Moore a chance for more publicity. About all the Bush team can do is attack Moore personally and say he is un-American.

The bottom line is that, amazingly, Moore has become a player in the election. We first reported on him during General Clark's campaign with his powerful comment on "The General and the Deserter." Now with his eye for satire and millions pouring into the bank, can the sequel to this movie be far behind.

Moore may impact the election by getting many new and traditional non-voters interested in the election. They go to movies every week and after watching Fahrenheit 9/11 (and little else political) may try a new activity in November, voting.

Politics sure is fun. Just wish the results wouldn't impact our lives so much.

## THE GRILL CAN WAIT
## JULY 3, 2004

Independence Day is the time to fly the flag and think about how lucky we are to be American citizens and how united we are in wanting our country to lead the world in the right direction. Hopefully, with that in our hearts, we will keep our minds open to other views and understand that in a democracy we can only have one president.

Our three branches of government are painfully far from perfect, but it is the best we have been able to do. The system must be corrected from within or we will lose our democracy. In the meantime, use today to reflect and teach your children how fortunate they are to be able to celebrate an Independence Day and how important it is to be an active informed citizen.

Then it is time to fire up the grill and have some fun.

## LET'S HOPE GUATEMALA IS NOT
## A ROLE MODEL FOR IRAQ
## JULY 7, 2004

The new Iraqi Government faces a tough road in trying to stop the fighting. How tough? Well here is a story that we have followed for 50 years.

Back in June of 1954 we were worried about President Arbenz's communist leaning government in Guatemala so we started a revolution and installed a friendly regime. The strange part was that hardly anyone in our country knew or cared. It was not reported in the papers or on television.

Well the people of Guatemala did care and the battles went on till 1996 when the government and the rebels signed a peace accords that's right, a 42-year war with over 200,000 people killed. (If you need a numerical perspective Guatemala has a population of 14 million and the equivalent number of U.S. killed would be 4,000,000)

Last month the Associated Press wrote about this war but we doubt that any more people cared today than they did in 1954. In any event, the Guatemalan rebels didn't have a trained army or many weapons so you can imagine the dangers of a prolonged battle in Iraq.

Maybe the only lesson that we should learn is that it is easier to start a war than to end one.

## THROWING ROCKS AT DEAD BEAVERS
## JULY 11, 2004

It is both funny and sad listening to the Senate Committee, the President, the Congress, the press and everyone else piling on the CIA. After this long investigation the Senate seems to have determined that the CIA is to blame for not preventing 9/11 and leading us into this whole Iraqi mess. Everyone up for reelection has been "misled." This is OK if you like theatre and don't take the show seriously.

The simple truth is the Congress will be the last to know how effective or ineffective the CIA has been. The President had to have a fall guy so he fired George Tenet. Now everyone has a nice clear target to focus on sort of like the old western saying, "Throwing Rocks at Dead Beavers."

Our guess is that the CIA is very effective but prefers for the enemy to think they are idiots. However, the politicians should be careful. If they throw "too many rocks" the CIA might fight back and have more agents in the White House than in Iraq.


## THE HEALTH CARD GETS COMPLICATED
## JULY 13, 2004

Several months ago we reported that the Vice President would use his heart condition as an excuse to quit the race and make it easier for Bush to win. At this time, Cheney seems ready to run and using his Doctor would not be so easy since we now know that the Doctor has been a drug addict for years. The new doctor might not be so easy to influence.

Some Democrats would like to get an official statement on Cheney's health, but that opens a Pandora's Box. First Cheney on the ticket is a big plus for Kerry and then the Republicans might ask for an official statement of Kerry's health since they are emphasizing how unprepared Edward's is to be President. But

Kerry's health problems probably result from Agent Orange exposure in Viet Nam and that would bring his service to the country back to center stage.

Don't know how it will play out, but aren't you glad you aren't a strategist advising either party.


## TWENTY FIRST CENTURY CAPITALISM ON TRIAL
## JULY 15, 2004

We hope that the public is not distracted by the Martha Stewart sentence (tough or easy) to believe that this is an example of our Justice Department's war on crooked capitalists. A hundred years ago Robber Barons ran some of our largest industries but in the 1990s a new more vicious mutant came alive. We reported on them in earlier Updates, but they brought thievery to a new level and with new skills to avoid responsibility. They set out to steal the country and their greed had no bounds. Their goal was to get a billion in the bank and if worse came to worse spend five or ten years in jail. Not a bad deal. The odds are great.

Many Americans and people throughout the world do not understand Capitalism. They are watching to see how cases of Enron and other leading companies that stole from thousands of people all over the world are handled. In the case of Ken Lay they will have to wait three or four years and after the election to see the decision. But if these 21st Century Robber Barons don't at least do the jail time of an idiot who holds up a bank, capitalism will take a big step back. Our economy, stock market and dollar will pay the price.

Martha is a fall girl people know her while they don't know Ken Lay. She is guilty but their crimes cannot be compared any more than a Little League player to Babe Ruth.

# The Conventions

## DEMOCRATS OFF TO A GOOD START
## JULY 26, 2004

The show was well produced and managed. Gore did well and Hillary was up to her usual level of effectiveness. But the heavy hitters were the former Presidents. Carter sounded the alarm about Bush saying, "Our country's soul was at stake." The party didn't want this type of attack since it could offend the undecided voter, but no one can doubt Carter's sincerity or knowledge.

Then the master hit on all cylinders. Clinton could sell videotapes for teaching public speaking. He has it all: brains, analysis, message and delivery. "They need a divided America, we don't" and "Strength and wisdom are not opposing values" will be used for decades. Love him or hate him, no one should miss a chance to listen to him talk. But you have to feel sorry for Kerry; it is a tough act to follow.

The only failing grades go to the press. The coverage was poorly planned and poorly executed. Boring and thoughtless are the kindest words we can say for CNN, CNBC, ABC, CBS and NBC.

Several months ago the Update reported on the Illinois Senate Candidate, Barack Obama. We said in a couple years he would be a national power. Well a funny thing happened on the way to the election. Kerry met Obama and lo and behold tomorrow night he is giving the keynote address. A star will be born.

## NIGHT OF THE IMMIGRANTS
## JULY 27, 2004

The second night of the convention was supposed to be quiet. It was not. The cable giants continued with their mediocre coverage. Public television tried their best. And the major networks faced a difficult decision..."The Last Comic Standing" won and they didn't spend a minute of their public airways time to lead or teach. (Newt Minow, where are you now that we need you.) Well for those of you that missed the show we will try to cover it briefly:

Howard: Undaunted

Ted: Vintage

Barack: Historic

Ronald: Et Tu Brute

Teresa: "Smart and well informed, just like men"

Barack and Teresa brought immigration to a new level. Two powerful American stories.


## SHOUTS, VETERANS AND SMILES
## JULY 28, 2004

Day three of the convention featured Sharpton launching rockets at the White House but the fun was watching commentators on CNBC losing their cool, cutting his speech off the air and launching personal attacks on him. Guess they forgot to pretend to be reporters. In any event it was what everyone expected from Sharpton and he did his usual loud and powerful delivery. If the Kerry team wanted to play it cool, they should have hid Al in an afternoon session.

The powerful part of the evening was the parade of famous Generals who are supporting Kerry or to be honest just trying to get rid of Bush. Michael Moore brought the issue of the "General and the Deserter" into the campaign months ago and though the Democrats said they would not focus on this issue, they are spending half of their time talking about Kerry's service. Max Cleland will serve double duty as he introduces Kerry tomorrow. First he will again bring up the Band of Brothers who fought for their country and probably Kerry will then comment on the dirty Republican campaign that called this triple amputee a traitor. Hope this campaign will be the final battle of Viet Nam.

Finally, Edwards played it cool. No attacks, just an average talk delivered very effectively and with a great smile. Elizabeth and their family were made for politics and she will be an effective campaigner. By contrast, Theresa is going to have to be managed carefully. She is a powerful woman ready to speak her mind at a moment's notice, not the best type of campaigner. Republican operatives will be planting mines all around her.

## MY NAME IS JOHN KERRY AND I AM REPORTING FOR DUTY JULY 31, 2004

This was first and most effective line from Kerry's acceptance speech.

We were a little nauseated by the constant repetition of his service in Viet Nam but I guess in politics you have to repeat something 200 times before voters get the idea that he fought and Bush didn't. Instead of Max Cleland and the Band of Brothers (which are from his history) he would have been better served to be introduced by General Clark and the dozen Generals and Admirals who were on the convention program (they are from the present war). Remember the election will be about Bush, but the voters want to be assured that Kerry can defend our country.

The networks deserve the blame for covering only one hour, but Kerry's advisors should have cut the content by 15 minutes no matter how important the subjects were. They forced Kerry to race through the speech. That said it was an effective talk with the big problem being too many promises that he won't be able to keep.

The rest of the evening was uneventful except General Clark showed why he would have been the stronger VP candidate and the Kerry girls showed they could teach their dad a thing or two.

Kerry and many speakers hit Bush hard. They have not reached the level of the" Republican Propaganda Machine" but there is little hope that the two sides will want to debate the issues. It will be blood and guts and since Kerry said he knows how to fight, he will get his chance. We can't wait till the Republican Convention.

Knowing that our Updaters are a brilliant group of observers, we would like to know what you thought of Kerry's chances coming out of Boston. Let us hear from you on a scale of 1 -5 with 1 equaling loser and 5 standing for champion.

## DON'T CHANGE HORSES IN MIDSTREAM
## AUGUST 3, 2004

This was the campaign slogan in the first presidential elections that we observed Franklin Roosevelt in 1940 and 1944. They say the Lincoln used the same approach but this was even before our time.

However, this year it seems that Bush is betting his Presidency on the fact that there is a terrible danger and he is the one to handle it saying do not change leaders in the midst of a war. Kerry is agreeing we are in danger but that's why we need him to lead us rather than the guy that got us into this terrible situation.

There is plenty of historical support for both of these positions. Roosevelt won both bitter elections even though when he died Harry Truman seemed to finish the war very effectively. And then of course Truman decided to get off the horse due to the Korean War and did not run for reelection and Johnson did the same in Viet Nam.

At the present time this matter is a rhetorical question. But with an attack before the election likely, how our country will react is the burning question. Will we blame Bush and elect Kerry or will be support Bush to let Al Qaeda know that they cannot control our election. This is the question.

## OBAMA HAS THE TABLE SET AS ILLINOIS GOP OUT SOURCES THEIR SENATE CANDIDATE AUGUST 5, 2004

Up to this week Barack looked like he was going to run against a weak and under financed Republican candidate but now the GOP is going all out to stop Obama before he becomes a national force. It looks like they will outsource the job to one of the best-informed and effective campaigners in the country Alan Keyes of Maryland. Obama will win but this will make the campaign a lot of fun. The debates will be classic and the country will be watching two highly intelligent black candidates one liberal and one conservative. Keyes has much more experience but if Obama handles him, his national stock will sky rocket. Doubt if an ambitious State Senator could have asked for anything more.

# LET'S GIVE THE "UNDECIDED" A REST AND INVITE SOME NEW FRIENDS TO THE PARTY
## AUGUST 10, 2004

We are getting tired of chasing the "undecided" voters. The analysis can make you crazy. For example some people don't like to declare their party and feel that politics is very personal. Then there are GOP business people that might vote for a change because they don't like Bush's economic policies but don't want to tell anyone about it. Then there are strong Democrats who believe we can't change horses in the midst of a war. And a lot of Army and National Guard families might be looking for a new policy in Iraq. Some Republicans are worried about Bush's ability to lead the country and certainly Kerry was almost no one's first choice. Then after all that we have to worry about how oil and the economy will affect the undecided

If all this sound confusing just be happy you are not Bush and Kerry spending tens of millions to influence this unusual group. They probably do not represent more than five percent and if in the end they break 60/40 it means a gain of just 1% overall

We think it is time to change our focus from the Undecided to the Unknown. Up to 50% of the eligible voters did not vote in the last Presidential election. The nonvoter figures on young educated men in their 20's is staggering raising all sorts of questions about our society and education system but here is a group that might be encouraged to cast their vote and could decide the election.

In the February 15, 2004 Update, Cousin David said his personal goal was to get fifteen new voters (in the hopes that 10 will actually vote) to participate in the election. His plan is beginning to sound better and better. If Bush and Kerry would spend their millions trying to educate and involve the 45% of the possible voters who still don't know what a democracy is, it would pay bigger dividends for them and it might be the best thing each of us can do for the next two months.

Actually, our two parties do not make it easy to vote and do not encourage these non-voters. But look at it this way, you will be doing the job their high school civics teacher tried and failed to do.

One final thought. Were you ever lonely and someone invited you to a nice party? Did you forget that person? We doubt it. Let's invite some new people to the election. Who knows they may turn out to really enjoy the party and thank you!

P.S. The tally on how Kerry did at the convention was not very conclusive. Only 14 of our highly informed readership responded and their grade was 4.2 on a scale of 1 to 5. Our thanks to those that did participate; but now we know how A. C. Nielsen feels when we don't answer their survey calls.

## THE ADVENTURES OF ABU GHRAIB BUT DON'T WORRY, THE HAPPY ENDING IS COMING NEXT WEEK AUGUST 19, 2004

When we were young (no comments please) we went to the movies on Saturday afternoon. The movies were fine but what we really went for was to see the serials to find out how our heroes escaped the terrible situation they were in at the end of the previous week's episode.

Therefore, early in life we realized that Hollywood Screen writers had a fantastic imagination and absolutely no shame. But little did know that we were being educated about how to review Congressional Committees and Military investigations. In May and June we reported on the Abu Ghraib mess and the blame was going right up to the Pentagon, Secretary of Defense and even the President.

Now the report is coming out with thousands of pages of infor- mation and hundreds of interviews. Boy the Pentagon must be sweating. But never fear. Remember the Hollywood writers they now work in Washington and you can be sure our heroes will escape without a scratch. Of course a few idiot soldiers and National Guard officers might take a fall, but if (and we do mean if) they plead guilty they will get off easy. And if things really get bad we may have to reprimand a couple Colonels and maybe a one star but this is war and they will have to settle for a smaller retirement check each month.

Just like the Saturday serials, no one really believed how the hero escaped, but it was fun to watch. So don't miss reading the report next week. Get a bag of popcorn and have a laugh. The Hollywood writers would probably be jealous.

## YOU HAVE TO GIVE THE PRESIDENT AN A PLUS FOR GUTS AUGUST 21, 2004

Of all the battles that you would think Bush would avoid it is about service in Viet Nam. But he is willing to take the curves at 80 miles an hour to win the election. There are three good reasons why he is taking on Kerry over this issue.

First Kerry was making headway in comparing his service compared to Bush and Cheney's avoidance of service in Viet Nam.

Second the Viet Nam Anti War debate rages on decades after you would think the wounds would have healed. Our country is not only divided over Iraq but still over the Viet Nam War. Kerry's anti-war position after he was discharged is still a hot button with the veterans who want to believe that their service was not in vain, a position that is easy to understand. For many, the war goes on.

Finally, Bush has been successful in turning military heroes into fools as he did with McCain and Max Cleland. And if you have a plan that has worked so well why quit. It is difficult saying with a straight face that he has not seen the commercials and knows nothing about them, but he toughs it out.

But the real reason we give the President an A plus for Guts is that the whole thing can so easily turn on him. First because the public was fooled with the same trick before and may get smarter. In addition some Republicans may have a weak stomach and attack the President. McCain's comments were just an example.

In the meantime, the Bush plan is kicking ass on all cylinders. Kerry is off message and his important plans are nowhere to be heard. Edwards has absolutely no news coverage. And the press spends all their time rebroadcasting the Swift Boat message. The public is confused which is just where Bush wants them to be.

Obviously this is not battle between respected politicians. It is closer to a duel.

Bush knows how to fight this type of battle. Kerry says he does, but so far he is still playing by the Marquis of Queensberry rules. Soon he will start shooting at the heart instead of the feet and it will get even uglier.

## WHAT A DICHOTOMY!
## AUGUST 25, 2004

While the United States is fighting for fair and honest elections all over the world, there is a growing fear, by both parties, that our November election will be filled with fraud.

An amazing comparison occurred this month. Jimmy Carter and international observers went to Venezuela to monitor the hard fought Presidential referendum. The key to their certification was that there was a paper trail even on the modern electronic voting machines. The monitor's randomly selected and hand recounted 7% of the precincts. This international support may have avoided a revolution.

By contrast, a very fast growing group of Americans believe that the "other side" will steal the presidential election. Both parties are training thousands of poll watchers and lawyers to monitor the process. The results in many close states may be challenged. Can you imagine 5 or 10 Florida's?

Lots of states still have outdated equipment and others have the new electronic voting machine (which 50 million of us will use). The concern is can the electronic machines be corrupted by the manufacturers (two of which are owned by powerful Republicans) or computer experts. Many groups have asked for a paper trail on the machines but that is probably not going to happen.

How ironic, the Venezuelan machines had a paper trail and our models do not.

Can our democracy survive another election like the last one? Can the "winner" govern if the election is contested across the country? Can the Supreme Court be put into another situation to decide the election and survive with any moral authority?

Maybe President Carter should invite President Chavez to monitor our election.

Oh my, remember the good old days when we only worried about hanging chads.

## SO MANY PROBLEMS WITH ONE SIMPLE SOLUTION FROM KING GEORGE
## AUGUST 27, 2004

Problem Number One: Not enough soldiers to run the war in Iraq. Back in the old days our Army was self-sufficient. They peeled their own potatoes and scrubbed their own latrines, fixed their own equipment and even drove their own supply trucks. And it worked well. But today we hire "contractors" to do everything from fix the trucks to interrogate prisoners.

Problem Number Two: Too many wars to cover. We have to keep rotating soldiers in and out of the country. We will need to keep a military force in Iraq for years The President is suggesting that we bring everyone home from Europe and Korea so they will not have to go from Iraq to Germany to Korea without coming home.

Problem Number Three: Tough to keep important suppliers like Halliburton happy. They have "billed billions", but are not happy with the profits and pissed off about disputes with the Inspector General some nonsense about overcharging six million a day and six billion unaccounted for. We better think it through. If Halliburton gets mad they might go home and we would be in deep dodo. We could afford to lose our "Coalition of the Willing" (after all they are only doing 10% of the fighting, but could not survive if Halliburton went home.)

Are you ready? All we have to do is study history. When King George III had a similar problem in the Revolutionary War he hired the Hessians to fight for him in the Colonies. It is the simple solution: we already have up to 100,000 civilian contractors involved in the war, why not get a quote from Halliburton on the cost of privatizing the entire occupation.

It is a modern business procedure you know, outsourcing.

Of course it would be a big bill with the cost of labor (soldiers) going up 10 or 20 times, but we wouldn't have to worry about starting the draft, news programs counting the dead, Geneva Convention violations, election distractions etc., etc., Think about it. No body except their family is concerned about the contractors. If they are killed some insurance company may pay the bill, but you don't have to give out medals or have lifelong medical care for the wounded. They are lining up every week to get the $100,000 jobs driving a truck. No telling how many would rush to join the new Halliburton Army.

After all, we are a capitalist country so what's wrong with outsourcing. And listening to all the war news is getting to be a drag. Halliburton is ready wonder what "our" King George might think.

# IF THE SPY RUMORS ARE CORRECT, SOMEONE GOOFED
## AUGUST 29, 2004

The U.S. spies on Israel and Israel spies on the U.S. We are close allies but still want to know everything that is going on. Hopefully it doesn't again reach the stage where it turns into deadly battles like the Israeli attack on our spy ship. Normally a spy getting caught is part of the game Jonathon Pollard can tell you all about it.

What makes this rumored case more serious is that Arabs see Israel and the US working together in their Middle East policy. In this case the" spy" worked for leaders in the Defense department who also were Jewish. Their honesty is not in question, but even the appearance of cooperation on secret plans regarding Iran is just what the Arabs fear. The story may be small in the U.S., but it will be a big story in the Middle East and among Anti-Semitic organizations.

If the story is true, it should never have happened and someone goofed in Tel Aviv and the Pentagon.


# CONVENTION MISCONCEPTIONS
## AUGUST 29, 2004

There are two popular misconceptions about the conventions. One was that the Boston convention was critical for Kerry to sell himself to the Democratic Voters. Two, the Republican Convention will be window dressing for the Republicans. Both were wrong and in fact reversed.

The Democrats throughout the country were in an "Anybody but Bush Mode" and Kerry's convention didn't have much impact. The pundits will be equally wrong if they think that the New York convention is a slam-dunk for Bush. A critical part of his base is worried. The Grand Old Party Conservatives live in fear of the deficits facing the country. The Regan Democrats are worried about their jobs and want to be convinced that the Bush Team knows what they are doing on the economy. The Warrior Wing is wondering if Bush has a plan to win in Iraq. The Bush Team has to show that they have the vision, the plans and the leadership to get the job done.

In effect the election will still be a referendum on the President with Kerry being the "other" guy. Only the committed voters follow the conventions more than an hour of two on TV. The rest of the potential voters are still more interested in reading about the new "Apprentice" show. Maybe Donald Trump should have run for President.

This is an important convention. Enjoy the show.


## ONE, TWO, BANG THREE
## AUGUST 30, 2004

Once again the networks ignored the convention. If the public makes an informed decision in November it certainly won't be due to their efforts.

The Republicans got off to a great start and Kerry is lucky it was not on the networks. Despite five hundred thousand demonstrators they were able to put on an effective performance.

Karl Rove as usual is way ahead of Kerry's team. Kerry says he will fight back but keeps expecting a gentleman's duel. Karl Rove did the proverbial "let's count to three and fire'. You could see from the presentations tonight that Rove aimed straight for the heart. It remains to be seen if Kerry is capable of fighting this type of vicious battle.

Only mistake (but fun) was Senator McCain calling out Michael Moore. It brought the movie's charges back into the news and probably will be worth another 20 million to Moore.

Stay tuned. It will be an exciting week.

## MONDAY'S OPENING ACT WAS TOO GOOD
## AUGUST 31, 2004

so today's speakers had a tough time getting started. Too bad because they had an important job. It's good for the Republicans that the first speakers were not on the network, which gave us only one hour of coverage. It would have been better for Karl Rove to switch Monday and Tuesday's program.

Senator Frist looked like he had a hard time believing himself about the success of the Republican health program. Senator Dole had a great presentation of the Republican platform, but she was preaching to the choir. Lt. Gov. Steele of Maryland might have had a powerful talk on civil rights, but the audience and the cable shows seemed bored so we don't know what he had to say.

Prime time Arnold gets an A for acting and a C for content. He didn't score any points and the constant camera shots of his famous Democratic wife didn't help.

With this said, it was up to Mrs. Bush to carry the ball, and she did. Who would have imagined that she would be one of the tough, effective and heavy hitting campaigners? Obviously, she is a great asset to the President, especially when compared to Mrs. Kerry.

Rioting in the street and death throughout the Middle East did not help the Convention or the headlines tomorrow. Hope that the speakers tomorrow can get across the domestic plans, if not George will have all the pressure on him Thursday. He is running as a wartime President, but lack of success in Iraq plus the lack of a domestic agenda could present a big problem.

# REPUBLICANS IGNORE DOMESTIC ISSUES AND RUN ON WAR
## SEPTEMBER 1, 2004

We expected that one night of the Convention would be devoted to talking about domestic plans, but hardly a word so far. Obviously, Karl Rove is confident that they can win on the defense of America, and the third act went on with a rather bland performance.

The show started with a tribute to President Reagan. The movie was terrific but we felt almost as sorry for Michael Reagan as we did for the Bush girls yesterday. Let's just say it is tough being the son of the "Great Communicator."

Milt Romney would have been perfect to bring home domestic issues, but instead they had him repeat the Anti-Kerry agenda. It was surprising to see him talking about the war with the history of his famous father being in a similar dispute.

Zell Miller is tough to evaluate. The crowd loved him and he certainly gave Kerry both barrels. He may well appeal to some Southern Democrats and if so Karl will have made a brilliant decision. Our guess is he may have turned off a similar number of Republicans. We would not have picked him to be tonight's only prime time speaker besides the Vice President.

What can we say about Cheney? As you know we were sure he would have been dumped from the ticket. He is tough to like and has so much baggage, but George Bush is very loyal to his friends. The Vice President is a poor speaker and his talk was unmemorable. Seems to us that it is up to George to carry the ball to victory tomorrow. After tonight he is sure to look great.

One suggestion to the Grand Old Party: give up the term: "and we honor him for his service." It becomes funny or worse Webster will soon have a new meaning for it. You can guess.

# THE PRESIDENT CARRIES THE BALL
## SEPTEMBER 2, 2004

The convention is over. It was very successful; however, it would have been even better if they eliminated the second and third day of the convention and went right from day one to tonight. Last night the Viet Nam War was replaced by the Civil War. The crowd loved Miller, but the country is the loser. Hatred will now explode with more lies and more smears. It will be tough for the winner to govern.

The set was dramatic (President in the round) and everything ran smoothly even the balloons. After General Frank's speech, the spotlight went on New York Governor Pataki introducing the President. He did well but don't believe he helped his bid for the nomination in four years. However, we may be prejudiced because we are looking for a Constitutional amendment that would limit Yale "Men" from being President more than three terms in a row.

The Presidential movie was weak, but it is tough to find something good to tell about the Bush until he got married. They all try for the success of "Man from Hope" but Clinton had better material.

The President was great. Looked terrific, confidant and certainly the speechwriters should get the Pulitzer Prize. Most important he delivered it like a leader. Once again, after a total rehash and renaming of existing or long discussed programs (without a mention of cost), he returned to being the War President, a theme he would like to stay on through November.

One note, the President went over the network time limit (10 PM) and the networks did not cut him off. We don't think they would have cut off Kerry, but he thought so and rushed his speech.

As we go into the final phase of the campaign, the Bush has the lead. The Swift Boat ads damaged Kerry and the Republicans will probably now back off from this viscous political attack. The economy and the war are helping Kerry and Nader is off the ballot in several key states. Lots to watch. Lots to think about. Let us hear from you.

What fun.

## THE WORLD IS WATCHING
## SEPTEMBER 5, 2004

Each year communication improves. This week we saw and understood the tragedy in Russia on CNN and they saw our political conventions on CNN.

When we were young we heard Hitler's speeches on the radio and it was scary. We later saw some news films at the movie theatre, but it had nowhere near the scope and impact of us watching children being shot in the back running out of the school or Russian people watching the Democratic and Republican Conventions. Our thoughts will have an impact on how Russia deals with Checknya and their view of our conventions will have an impact on how they support our country's policies.

What our politicians say about each other will make a big difference in whether or not other countries support the one that wins. Kerry tried to limit the personal attacks at the convention. Karl Rove doesn't care what happens if Kerry wins.

Right now we are headed off a cliff. Kerry's supporters are demanding that he trash the President. Bush has little international support to begin with and if Kerry responds with the hate that was directed at him, the other countries will feel they made the right decision to sit on the sidelines more or less a plague on both your houses.

It is a sad day when politics overwhelms critical national interest. The world is watching.

## IT IS THE FATHER WHO SHOULD EXPLAIN
## SEPTEMBER 8, 2004

The Viet Nam War goes on. Today's attack on the President's service in the Air National Guard is an old story and one that we commented on many months ago. Michael Moore was supporting General Clark and dubbed the campaign a battle between the "General and the Deserter." We expected that the story would have legs and come back into the campaign but today have another thought.

Iraq and Viet Nam have many things in common. The saddest was that wealthy and influential families found ways for their children not to be on the wall in Washington and the same is happening in Iraq. We think you have to look at the parents who assisted or encouraged their children to avoid service.

In this case it is Bush 41 that should be questioned. We know what Bush 43 was interested in at the time, but without his father's influence he would have been drafted (going to Canada was not an option for a Congressman's son). And then you have to think long and hard about a person who is officially sending other young men to fight and die while protecting his own son.

This is a tough subject to write about. You have to ask yourself what you did or what you would have done. But tonight the facts are easy to understand. The questions should not be directed at the son, but the father. It is important that we learn from the past.

## A ROSH HASHANAH PRAYER THAT
## HAD SPECIAL MEANING TODAY
## SEPTEMBER 16, 2004

During today's Jewish New Year Service a traditional prayer seemed to be especially moving. It goes like this:

For Our Nation and Its Rulers

We pray for all who hold positions of leadership and responsibility in our national life. Let your blessing rest upon them, and make them responsive to your will, so that our nation may be to the world an example of justice and compassion.

Deepen our love for our country and our desire to serve it. Strengthen our power of self-sacrifice for our nation's welfare. Teach us to uphold its good name by our own right conduct.

Cause us to see clearly that the well-being of our nation is in the hands of all its citizens: imbue us with zeal for the cause of liberty in our own land and in all lands: and help us always to keep our home safe from affliction, strife, and war. Amen.

And boy do we hope our prayers were heard.


## GETTING PAST RATHER
## SEPTEMBER 18, 2004

The President's National Guard Service is an old story that has never been refuted. His Father got him in to an Air National Guard unit that was filled with sons of privilege, a unit that was sure not to be sent to Viet Nam. For a Bush getting into the unit was no harder than getting into Yale. Life is one of privilege if you are a Bush, Kennedy or thousands of elite families. Some of their sons wanted to serve their country, but thousands of others used deferments, phony physical ailments, the National Guard and if all else failed, Canada to avoid Viet Nam.

George completed his flight training and then asked to be transferred to an Alabama unit so he could work on a political campaign. No one remembers him attending any training sessions in Alabama and it seems he just blew it off knowing that his father would take care of any problem. He also was discharged early so he could go to Harvard. The President has never denied this and every strong supporter who is now attacking Rather knows these facts.

With this in mind it is amazing that CBS got involved in the story and in effect become the story. It may have been stupidity on their part, a brilliant Republican plot, or some confusion that may be cleared up. But it is a non-story because everyone who wants to know already knows the facts. We don't need any more time wasted on how Kerry or Bush served their country thirty years ago.

But the attack on Rather is a serious diversion from what leading Republicans and Democrats call a disaster in Iraq and an economic calamity facing our country. Neither Kerry nor Bush has a clue what to do and treat us like fools telling us that they have a plan. They are both acting like the Wizard in the Land of Oz.

The election will decide who will be in the White House, but not how our country will get out of the Dog House. We will have to choose between the man who got us into this disaster and the one who is wondering if he can get us out.

Hopefully we will see who is really behind the curtain during the debates.

# The Clem Kadiddlehopper Effect

## NEW UPDATER CHECKS IN
## SEPTEMBER 22, 2004

It is not often we publish a letter to the Update as an individual message but this one seems of particular importance because Clem Kadiddlehopper is one of those "new" voters and a guy who is learning about the political process. Clem sent this email today:

---

*Thanks for the updates. They are real interesting and I was looking forward to the debates you were talking about so I went to write the dates on my calendar. Well you can imagine my surprise, the first one on the 30th was the same time as a San Francisco Giant game and you know how important it is to watch them and make sure they lose. And the other three debates conflict with the play-off games that I am sure the Cubs will be in. This is our year!!!! I was really upset. They had the whole summer to hold these debates why put them on during the most exciting baseball games.*

---

*But today I hear some good news. Fox News - that fair and balanced TV station - is not going to interrupt their baseball schedule for the debates. They said we have all heard the President speak a lot so it is not so important and better yet, during the game they will give us little reports on how well the President is doing. I'll bet they are Cub fans too. So I will be able to watch the Cubs win the World Series and still be an intelligent voter in November. But I do have to call and see about registering.*

*Keep them updates coming. I like the email.*

*Sincerely,*

*Clem Kadiddlehopper*

---

## THE MOST INTERESTING NEW VOTING BLOCK
## SEPTEMBER 26, 2004

In the past the military rarely had a chance to question their leaders. They were ordered to fight and fight they did but today there are new elements.

First the demographics have changed. There are young soldiers who in Viet Nam and previous wars did not have the right to vote. This is the first time 18 to 21 year olds who are fighting have had this opportunity.

Second, there are more mature family soldiers. The large numbers of National Guard troops have brought older soldiers and their immediate families into the electoral process as never before. They are a powerful group in many states.

The next group is the professional soldiers. Many leading retired Generals and Admirals are supporting Kerry and some Bush but they all lived through Korea and Viet Nam and know the devastating effect on the soldiers they commanded. We don't remember this type of split in the past. (Of course the ones that are on active duty are wisely cautious about expressing opposition.)

A vote for Bush will obviously mean that we stay the course. We have been through this with Harry Truman and Lyndon Johnson. It took a new President to change the course Eisenhower to stop the fighting in Korea and Nixon (after a long time) to get out of Viet Nam. The career military is in the best position to know if they are succeeding or failing. To put it bluntly, they know if the war is worth their men and women dying for.

Finally there are the future military families. If the war continues we will have a draft. The world is a tinderbox and if the Iraq war continues (under Bush or Kerry) a draft is inevitable. Sort of like taxes the subject is taboo for both sides till after the election. Many voters who have a son or daughter over 16 will be thinking about the prospect for a draft and will have to decide if Bush or Kerry would be best for their family and their country.

Absentee Ballots are flooding into the states from military families around the world. We are very proud of our all-voluntary military and it will be interesting to sell how they vote on their future. In a close election they could end up being the voting block that picks the next President.

If it works out that way, it would be very fitting.

## GOOD NEWS FROM CLEM
## SEPTEMBER 29, 2004

Everyone is following the undecided voter and that is why we are so pleased that Mr. Kadiddlehopper is communicating his thoughts during the election cycle. (However please note that this email was written before the Cub loss and the San Francisco win yesterday):

---

*Well things are going well. The Cubs look like they are going to go all the way. The last two games took the pressure off me but you never know. I watched the Bear game Sunday to relax from the pressure, and wouldn't you know it they lost Grossman for the season. Oh well, I remember when they won the championship and no one in Chicago can remember when the Cubs won.*

*As for politics, there is big news. Thanks for all the encouragement and I did it. And it wasn't much. They registered me to vote and it only took a few minutes. But I guess that is where the tough part comes. For the past four elections, I didn't plan on voting so I didn't have to listen to the debates or make any decision. There are so many people running for office I think I will just concentrate on the two unusual guys running to be Senator and of course, the President.*

*Boy is they nasty. Sounds like neither of them are a very good person. When I just watched the speeches in the news the President sounded real strong, but now those Democrats are sure saying some bad things. Don't know what to think. If I had to make a choice today I would have to stick with Bush you can't let those terrorists get away with killing so many people in New York and the President kind of reminds me of Clint Eastwood and would know how to be tough. But I am worried about my job. Our plant is not doing too well and a lot of business comes from Motorola who are laying off a lot of people. Hope it doesn't affect me. Some of the guys in the plant say Kerry is better for us if we lose our jobs so I have to keep an open mind. I guess that is why you call me one of them undecided voters.*

*Thanks for all the suggestions. I am going to videotape the debates so I can watch all the important games and then watch the debates when we have time.*

*It is exciting thinking about picking the President, but it sure is a lot of work. I promise to write again soon.*

*Sincerely*

*Clem Kadiddlehopper*

---

# PRE DEBATE COMMENTARY
## SEPTEMBER 30, 2004

A few thoughts before the "big" debate:

1. *Lincoln and Douglas must be twisting in their graves watching two presidential candidates cheating democracy by refusing to have a meaningful debate on the issues facing our country.*

2. *The moderators and the news people asking the questions will control the debates and by and large determine the outcome. Will they press both candidates on the multitude of issues which need clarification? We doubt it and the debate may turn into a review of "the best sound bites of 2004" that we have all heard for the past six months.*

3. *The popular view is that Kerry has to score big and the Bush has to avoid any stupid comment. We don't agree. From the beginning this election has been a referendum on the Bush Presidency and it is Kerry who has to avoid making any stupid comment. If Kerry comes across as a reasonable, well-informed candidate, many of the undecided will vote against Bush.*

4. *Ignore the polls and the talking heads use your eyes and ears and let your brain do the thinking.*

Send us your thoughts. We will send ours later.

# The Debates

## THE REPORT CARD KERRY: A - BUSH: C - SEPTEMBER 30, 2004

If their old Speech Professor at Yale (both had the same one) were grading the debate, Kerry would have won. His posture, gestures, facial expression, timing etc. was superb. Bush had trouble in all these areas.

If you judge every question and the closing comment, Kerry won at least 15 and Bush won 1 with 4 being a draw. Everyone knows that Bush is not a strong debater but this was his key area and he didn't do a good job. We were surprised that he was not better prepared.

Kerry not only did not make any mistakes he delivered a strong message and presidential image that got stronger as the grueling debate continued. Bush obviously tired after the first hour and started to search for words. He frequently turned to using Republican attack slogans against Kerry, which didn't come off very well. He doesn't do as good a job as Rush.

With this said, it is hard to know how much of an effect it will have on the campaign. It should give Kerry a point or two in the swing states reenergize the Democratic workers, help with fund raising and make the next three debates more interesting and critical than anyone would have suspected.

Although some issues were clarified the only news was Kerry's indirect comment that we are building 14 permanent military bases in Iraq, which may tell us more about the future than all the other rhetoric.

Congratulations are in order for NPR's questions and handling of the debate although the formal structure sure leaves a lot to be desired.

## WELL HERE IS THE NEWS FROM CLEM OCTOBER 1, 2004

*I am really sorry. We were listening to the Cubs lose to the Reds (12 innings of pain) so after work the guys went out to have a beer and after three boilermakers I sort of lost track of the time. Anyway after I got home and dialed up the Giant game and they were winning, I kind of lost it. Forgot all about the debate.*

*I know you wanted to know what I thought about the debate so I listened to one of those talk radio programs on the way to work today and they said it was sort of a draw, so maybe I didn't miss anything. Anyway I circled the next debate - next Friday - and will be sure to get informed. I do apologize because I know the election is real important but the Cubs can make anyone crazy.*

## WHAT A DIFFERENCE A DEBATE MAKES
## THE PRESSURE IS ON THE PRESIDENT
## OCTOBER 3, 2004

The first debate influenced many more people than we expected. Now the polls are close and the pressure is on the President to improve his performance on Friday. It will not be easy because he has to defend his administration's record and has not answered any hostile questions in this campaign. On top of all that, his advisers must be pounding away with instructions not an enviable position.

The visual part of the last debate (where he could not control his facial emotions) may have hurt him more than the answers. My guess is that people saw the same indecisiveness that Michael Moore showed in his movie when the President was told we are under attack. It certainly was not presidential.

Kerry should have all the advantage in a debate about the economy (with no record to defend except his Senate votes), but in this election, who knows what will happen next.

In any event, many people will be watching the next debate to see if Bush just had a bad night or is just not on top of his game.

Sure makes politics fun.


## WEAR YOUR FLAK JACKET
## THE VP DEBATE WILL BE ROUGH, BUT FUN!
## OCTOBER 4, 2004

VP Cheney has the tough job of picking up the pieces after the President's debate so it is critical that he wins however, as tough and talented a person as is, he has a lot of baggage. First his record as VP (they will greet us with flowers) and former President of Halliburton is a challenge and his personality is not exactly made for TV. Last time our old friend Joe Lieberman was a patsy.

Edwards will not only come looking for a fight but will start one hoping to make the VP lose his cool. The Senator has to defend his inexperience to be President compared to the extensive experience by the VP, and of course the image of a trial lawyer. But it should be great. So enjoy the show but wear a Flak Jacket in case there is a stray bullet.

## SECOND GAME OF THE NATIONAL SERIES GOES TO EDWARDS 12 TO 5 OCTOBER 5, 2004

Edwards was extremely well prepared and delivered but both were tiring in the last 20 minutes (such as blowing the question on what's wrong with Flip-Flops). The moderator spent too much time on several questions but certainly challenged them with unusual and tough questions.

Our surprise was that Cheney wasn't better prepared. His body language was poor and he spent half the time talking to the table. Of course he had the tough job, a record to defend, not a theory on what could be.

If the President was counting on Cheney to pick up lost ground, he didn't and might have even lost another point or two. Will have to wait till tomorrow and see what the supporters say on morning TV and radio. When you hear someone talking fast and at an emotionally high sound level you will know his or her candidate lost!

Forecast: More pressure on Bush Friday.

# TWO PARTIES IN SEARCH OF AN EXIT PLAN
# OCTOBER 7, 2004

With the round of news about no WMD, insufficient troops, disastrous planning, increasing violence, etc., the pressure is on the President to tell us his exit plan and for Kerry to tell us how his plan differs from Bush. Tough job because neither has the courage to tell the truth. There are only a few choices, none of them good and like it or not, that is where our country is today.

But before we decide on the solution we should review the goals. In our opinion the President invaded Iraq for two reasons: control of oil and influence in the Middle East. Our relationship with Saudi Arabia was in trouble and they needed to get rid of our bases or face a revolution. If the supply of Middle East oil is used against us, our economy could collapse.

If you believe there are other reasons why we invaded Iraq please share them with us.

Now here are two widely discussed solutions plus one more from the Update:

1.  *Stay the Course: Bush says we just keep going until the new government can take over. This is difficult as more people are turning against us every day. Violence begets more violence and the average Iraqi blames us for bringing disaster to their homes.We probably will have to increase troop strength and destroy the opposition (think major battles and bombings to get the idea). Then we will have troops there till we can establish a "friendly" Sadam who will rule with our interests in mind. Of course it will be rough for our troops and for the Iraqis but some other President (Jeb or Hillary) will have to deal with it in four or eight years.*

2.  *Cut, Run and Pray: A position that has many supporters in Washington and around the world. Cousin David clearly presented this position in our Update last month. (If you didn't read it we will be pleased to forward a copy) It is also the*

*plan favored by thousands of knowledgeable people includ-
ing the Arch Conservative Pat Buchanan in his current book.
He called our war in Iraq the greatest foreign policy mistake
in our history and the sooner we withdraw the better. The
old "Declare Victory and Leave" policy will not help the inter-
im government, as they will be reserving their seats on the
helicopters right behind us. We will look like fools and will
have destroyed the lives of millions of Iraqis as civil war will
probably follow, but "you win some and you lose some."*

3. *Sign the Treaty and Step Back: This is the plan we have
written "around" for over a year and one that our leaders
may be working on. So how do we control the oil, influence
the Middle East and stop fighting in the cities. First we elect
a friendly government (January), then we negotiate long
term leases for U.S. bases in Iraq (think Guantanamo, Panama Canal, Philippines, etc.), and after a year or so of trying
to bring peace we retreat to the bases, give money and
wish them luck. In any event we control the flow of oil and
maintain military power in the Middle East.*

You have to feel sorry for Bush and Kerry. It is tough trying to be
honest in the middle of an election.


## THEY CAN BOTH SLEEP WELL TONIGHT
## OCTOBER 8, 2004

Bush and Kerry accomplished their goals. Bush showed that he
really can debate and Kerry continued to look Presidential. Tech-
nically Kerry won with more precise answers but still lacks the
warmth and skill that a Bill Clinton (also a Yale speech student)
exhibits in responding to questions. Bush fell off the cliff with the
final three questions on the Supreme Court, abortion and that
old perennial wrong decisions, but he had good humor, seemed
relaxed and probably prevented another drop in the polls. Our
guess is there won't be much change in the polls so they both
should consider the debate a success.

---

As a citizen we might not sleep as well because the debate showed two candidates telling fairy tales on taxes, draft, economy, etc and we don't even get warm milk.

## KERRY WINS, BUT BUSH DOES NOT LOSE
## OCTOBER 13, 2004

The President held his own on most issues but once again having to defend a record of action (or inaction) is tough and Kerry looked and talked Presidential. The three debates, won by Kerry, turned the election into a toss-up or more likely with a lead for Kerry. The Republicans seemed more hysterical in the spin room so it probably means they agree with us.

Unfortunately, the three formats were not very helpful or informative to the electorate. We hope in the future that the debate format will be standardized or decided long before the candidates are picked.

Now it looks like the long knives will come out. The character assassination in the next two weeks will probably make most voters sick to their stomach, but obviously for some, it will be the decisive factor in whether they vote and for whom.

Join Bush and Kerry in prayer for our democracy

## AN AMAZING TURN OF EVENTS: CLEM HELPS THE COUNTRY MAKE THE DECISION AND THANKS THE UPDATE FOR HELPING HIM BE AN EXPERT OCTOBER 13, 2004

*I want to thank the reader of your Updates that told the TV Station about me being undecided on who to vote for. Well they called me Monday and paid me $500 to watch the debate and do some research. I went to their station and they gave me this device where I needed to press one button if I liked what the President or the Senator was saying and one if I didn't like it.*

*Well I sort of liked everything they said, so I pressed a lot of the good button. Then they asked me if I had decided and I said no, so they are going to interview me next week to see if I have made a decision.*

*To be honest they both seemed nice and I would be happy to see either of them win.*

*Anyway it was nice getting paid for my opinion and I hope it helped their listeners.*

*Sincerely,*

*Clem Kadiddlehopper*

# The Last Two Weeks

## TWO WEEKS TO GO AND IT IS THE JOBS, STUPID! OCTOBER 19, 2004

Going into the final two weeks we would like to review two Updates that we wrote in January during the nomination process. First, we predicted that Kerry would be a weak candidate because so many people think "MassachusettsLiberal" is "one" dirty word. We also suggested that the election will be a referendum on President Bush and decided by a few voters in five or six swing states. Although Kerry was better than we thought, it looks like both comments are holding up.

For example, we made an indicator list to predict if President Bush would be reelected. We gave positive and negative points to Bush on everything from the war in Iraq (number of casualties), job creation, Dow Jones (at least 1100), oil (less than $40.) etc. Amazingly, today Bush does not have a single positive point yet he leads Kerry! And when you add that Kerry won all three debates including one where Bush was really mixed up, how could you explain this other than that Karl Rove is the most effective political mastermind in history or Kerry is a poor candidate in the eyes of the country.

The other thought was that there are only a "few who will choose." Forget the national polls; they are absolutely of no value. Who cares how many people in New York will vote for Kerry or how many Texans will vote for Bush. Watch only the polls in the swing states.

This time Bush may win the National vote total, but just as Gore, lose the election in the electoral college, Basically the loss of good factory jobs are bringing industrial states like PA, MI, OH, WI into the blue column. Kerry may not be able to bring their jobs back but they have lost faith that the President is trying. Florida is still the most critical state, but Kerry can win without it. We will review the swing states in a future Update but even small states like Colorado will play a big role (if the split vote amendment passes Kerry will get at least 4 votes in a Red State). It will be fun and you will need your adding machine.

For political junkies we suggest you go into training for sleepless nights on the 2nd, 3rd and 4th of November. And don't forget to refill your prescription for the blood pressure medicine you will need it!

## POLLSTERS STUDY CLEM, OUR OWN UNDECIDED VOTER OCTOBER 20, 2004

We heard from Clem and it seems the election is becoming a money machine. Here is the email we received:

---

*Well, it is amazing. The Zigzag Company wants to interview me to study my thought process in deciding who to vote for. They are going to show me a lot of statements by Kerry and Bush and I am supposed to rate every one. At the end I can look at my score and see whom I should vote for. They say it is a crash course in voting. And you won't*

---

*believe it; they are going to pay me $1,000 to let them study my ideas. Frankly, I never knew that my ideas were worth so much money.*

*I am going in when I have some time, right after the Yankee-Red Sox series that really is exciting. If the Red Sox can do it, I know the Cubs can next year.*

*So anyway, in a few days I will let everyone know who I am voting for. Like you said, politics are important but can also be fun. Glad I decided to be an undecided voter*

*Sincerely,*

*Clem Kadiddlehopper*

---

## THE CONVOLUTED VOTER
## OCTOBER 25, 2004

If you are voting for a candidate you believe is best for the country, consider yourself lucky. A good percentage of the voters are voting for a special interest or against someone or thing. For example:

1. *Half the votes for Kerry are really votes against Bush.*

2. *Many people are one-issue voters and that is all they care about.*

3. *Some voters want gridlock and are voting for Kerry so the country will have a Democratic President and a Republican Congress the result, nothing.*

4. *Some voters hate Bush but want to see him stuck with the mess he created.*

5. *Many are voting their pocketbook jobs or fewer taxes.*

We could go on and on but we do long for the old days when people just voted for the "best" candidate.

By the way everyone is talking about a repeat of 2000 with the results not known for days or weeks. That is terrible but there is one thing that would be worse a tie. 2 69 used to just be a sex term, but could become a joke on the country if each of the candidates get 269 electoral votes. What a headache as congress selects the next President and the country becomes more divided than ever.

Oh well, we will offer our prediction on Wednesday. Your thoughts are very welcome.


## CLEM DECIDES MAYBE!
## OCTOBER 25, 2004

Many Updaters have been waiting for Clem to make the big decision. It is rough being an undecided voter, but there is good news in this email from Clem:

---

*Well with Boston ahead by two games, I was able to relax and take time to go down to the election pollster's research lab.*

*They showed me film clips of the President and Senator making a lot of comments and studied my responses. Afterward they said that I would vote for President Bush. Frankly I liked both guys; they seem smart and know everything about running the country. Probably the most sensible thing that the President said was that it is better to fight in Iraq than in our own streets and you sure can't*

---

*argue with that. And like I told you Bush looks like a tough guy who knows how to handle himself.*

*But I didn't like that those pollsters were telling me how I would vote. It is supposed to be secret, isn't it? I might give it another thought before Election Day.*

*Well, they thanked me for taking part in the study and said it helps them determine how the election will turn out. They said a lot of the undecided voters are just like me, which made me feel good. They said to come to the studio on election night because Larry King might want to interview me. That is amazing. I guess I just became famous, all because I was undecided.*

*And it does take a lot of pressure off, I now know who I am supposed to vote for so I am ready for my first election and the money they paid me was a big bonus.*

*Thanks for your help in making me well known.*

*Sincerely,*

*Clem Kadiddlehopper*

---

# BAD NEWS AND MORE VOTERS =
# A NEW PRESIDENT
## OCTOBER 27, 2004

Time to put our chips on the line. It is easy to be a talking head on TV or a political hack that predicts his or her candidate will win when no one expects them to be honest. The Update may not be any more accurate but we will give you our honest opinion.

As we said reported earlier, it is amazing that bad news from all sides surrounds the President. You name it: war, draft, Supreme Court, stock markets, $50 oil, lack of jobs, less medical coverage, war crimes, flu vaccine, etc., etc., It is only a tribute to the poor candidacy of Senator Kerry that the race is so close.

The president has very strong supporters and a powerful media machine but the Kerry campaign has done a much better job of getting new voters involved. The turnout will set a record and that is great for our democracy; so get to the polls early and here is whom you will see in line:

1. *Traditional non-voters are excited about this election and in the key states the majority of them will vote for change. There are also simply more Democrat non-voters than Republican non-voters. Or another way to look at it, Republicans may routinely consider voting a duty so there are less new Republican leaning non-voters for the Bush team to bring to the polls*

2. *Registering and igniting new and young voters. Gov. Dean showed that the Internet could get the 18 to 29 year olds involved in the election and once again with all the bad news; they are more likely to vote for change.*

3. *The woman's vote is hard to interpret but they are coming out and Kerry seems to be getting the edge.*

4. *Black voters in key states felt that their Florida vote was not counted and will come out in record numbers with 85% going to Kerry.*

Republicans have done a great job with absentee ballots and that could be a sleeper in close races, but the Kerry's team just has more voters to work with. Of course just with Clem our own new voter, they have to show up on Tuesday.

Tomorrow we will predict how Kerry gets to 270 votes.

Stay calm and try to enjoy the excitement and drama.

## NYTIMES.COM: 2004 ELECTION GUIDE THINK OF IT LIKE A BIG PUZZLE—OR HOW KERRY WILL GET TO 270 ELECTORAL VOTES (PLUS A HANDY DO IT YOURSELF PUZZLE BOARD AT NO EXTRA COST) OCTOBER 28, 2004

This election is shaping up like a big puzzle so start like you normally do in the corners.

California in the Southwest corner and Washington and Oregon in the Northwest. Boy they fit perfectly. All of New England has a lot of pieces but they seem to fit together and really help get the picture started.

Now let's look at the other corner and see if we can find Florida Oh Oh, Florida seems to be missing so I guess we need to work on some other part of the country.

Let's go back up North where we found all those Blue New England States and add New York, New Jersey, Delaware, Maryland, and D.C. Boy they look like they were born in Blue.

Now it is time to work on the old Rust Belt Industrial States of Pennsylvania, Ohio and Michigan lot of lost jobs seem to make the pieces fall right in place.

Indiana must be broken because it doesn't fit, but wow, Illinois and those old liberal guys in Wisconsin and Minnesota look a little worn out but seem to almost jump into place.

Look at that the score card says Kerry wins with 272 votes.

Of course if we can find Florida it gets much easier, but there are other states that might come Kerry's way like a split in Colorado, Iowa (who for better or worse gave us Kerry), New Mexico, etc. but many of the Blue and Red states are simply up for grabs.

If you don't like our puzzle we are including the New York Times Calculator so you can play your own game. Click on Presidential Calculator and be your own Kingmaker. Let us know your score on how Bush or Kerry win.

We hate to mention it but our puzzle looks a little like a Civil War Map. Kerry's North and Pacific (Blue) against Bush's West and South (Red). Hope it is just a coincidence. Either way this will be a wild election and the President may lose but still win the popular vote as his support in most states is overwhelming. We guess he and Al Gore could have a beer over that one.

Place your bets and enjoy the action. This show only comes every four years.

Good luck to your candidate.

# CLEM ANNOUNCES HIS DECISION
# A SPLIT VOTE AND A GUILTY VERDICT
# OCTOBER 31, 2004

Here it is folks. The decision from our own Undecided Voter, Clem Kadiddlehopper:

---

*Well this is sure going to be a busy week. The election and the closing arguments on the Scott Peterson trial. I think he is guilty and even after listening to that famous defense attorney I think he just was fooling around too much and had a big fight with his wife. Probably the reason I never got married. Anyway I am looking forward to what happens. But today I am ready to become a decided voter.*

*With this Osama tape I think we have to support President Bush. But in the Senate race I am going for Obama. It is funny*
*I am against Osama but for Obama. Anyway this way I am voting for one Republican and one Democrat guess that is fair. I kind of feel good that I have made a decision and am no longer one of the undecided voters that everyone talks about and am looking forward to voting Tuesday night.*

*Thanks again for all your education. By the way I would sure like to hear from your readers if they agree with me that Peterson is guilty. As much as I listen about this case don't see how anyone could say he is innocent. Wonder if Larry King will cover the trial or the election Tuesday night. Tough decision, but I know the election is pretty important.*

*Sincerely yours,*

*Clem Kadiddlehopper*

## THOUGHTS ON ELECTION EVE
## OSAMA RIDES TO THE PRESIDENT'S
## RESCUE AT LEAST ON TAPE
## NOVEMBER 1, 2004

Republicans can thank Osama bin Laden for the perfect close to the campaign by emphasizing the President's strong point in the eyes of voters fighting against terrorism. It was such a great lob our guess is Karl Rove didn't even have to write out the marching orders to his attack team. It was easy quoting Michael Moore.

Our guess is that it will affect a few votes, but by and large the audience of the Rush Limbaugh's of the world is set in stone. The Ditto Heads are working with heart and soul for the President and the rest are listening for entertainment and are voting for Kerry. As far as the undecided well let's think about our friend Clem Kadiddlehopper he will be listening to reports from the Scott Peterson trial, not Rush or any political program.

By the way, the shrill attacks on Kerry make us think that the Bush team is very worried.

Are There Serious Defections in the President's Inner Circle?

The last two weeks have been filled with strange negative stories about the Bush team. And the stories came from Republicans, Big Business and Government Departments under Republican control. For example, the investigation of the NAACP (Republican IRS), the investigation of, Halliburton, (FBI and Justice Department), Layoffs in battleground states (by GM and other large corporations), Arms Depot Fiasco (by Generals), etc. etc. All these items could have been buried for a week until after the election. Our only conclusion is that many traditional Republican Supporters are afraid of Bush and are trying to sabotage him. We will probably hear more about this after the election.

How Can the Country Get Put Back Together?

This campaign was wild, bitter and crooked. That is OK and we have had terrible battles in the past. But this time it wasn't just the politicians that are emotional; this battle infected the hearts of the people. They view the opponent as a villain Bush as Hitler and Kerry as a Traitor. Even if the election runs smooth, which is a joke because they never do, the country will be impossible to put back together.

The fun part will be to see the people who fermented this hate now tell the losing party that they must join hands and all work together. It will not happen unless you can imagine Rush talking for three hours on how Kerry will be a great president or Michael Moore making a movie on why Bush should get the Nobel Peace Prize.

Hang in there.

# The Morning after

**UPDATE ACCURATELY PREDICTED THE RESULTS IN 49 OUT OF 50 STATES BUT WHAT A DIFFERENCE THAT STATE MAKES! NOVEMBER 4, 2004**

Ohio was devastating to Kerry, the only state the Update missed in our prediction of October 28th. He got 252 electoral votes and we predicted 272 with the difference being Ohio's twenty votes. Don't know of anyone who did a better job in predicting the outcome. It was not luck or skill there were only a few states that really were in play and that is the problem that the Democrats face. (More about that in a few days).

But first, Congratulations are due to President Bush. Karl Rove will go down in history as a political mastermind. He put together a coalition of unusual concerns and interests that overcame a Kerry team that was out thought and out tricked.

Our condolences to Senator Kerry, You might say he was: "The wrong man, in the wrong place, at the wrong time." We felt that before the nomination process but he did much better than we expected and in fact came within an inch of being elected. He just could not understand that he was in the middle of a civil war.

The President says he will "reach out to the other half of the country." but he might be reaching for their throat instead of their hand.

In fact we don't see how the President can meet his promises to his constituency and unite the country. An agenda of reducing gay rights and abortion forces him to appoint very conservative Supreme Court judges. So many promises to keep: winning the war in the middle east, more tax cuts, increasing the power of big business, reducing environmental programs, etc. does not sound like a compromise is possible. Lots of money and emotions were invested in Bush and his supporters are waiting for their reward.

Some commentators say that Bush will move to the center to create his spot in history, but we don't believe Bush worries about his place in history. He got a mandate with not only more Republicans in Congress but very conservative and inexperienced politicians. He also has rock solid Red State support and he intends to use it.

You might compare the President to a very tough and rich poker player who has 2 aces in the hole and the next card is another ace Do you think he will "check" to be nice to his opponents and if he did "check" you know a bigger trick is coming.

So much to think about. Whether you won or lost, it was an emotional ride. Take some time to relax and reflect and send us your thoughts.

## UPDATES TOP 10 REASONS BUSH WON NOVEMBER 6, 2004

1. *Karl Rove*

2. *Bush's Wife*

3. *Kerry's Wife*

4. *Swift Boat Veterans For Bush*

5. *Massachusetts Gay Marriage Judges*

6. *Evangelical Christians*

7. *Wall Street and Big Business*

8. *Latino and Jewish Voters*

9. *Catholic Bishops*

10. *John Kerry*

## CLEM TELLS US HOW IT IS
## NOVEMBER 7, 2004

Everyone has been waiting to hear from Clem to see how he enjoyed voting. And here is the latest word from our former own Undecided Voter.

---

*Well I am sort of ashamed to tell you this, but a funny thing happened. I got off work at 4:00 and listened to the radio while driving home. They had all sorts of predictions and said the*
*President was going to lose in Illinois so my vote couldn't help him, and that Barack Obama was going to win easily so he didn't need my vote.*

*Well I got to my polling place about 5 PM and lo and behold there was a long line. I guess the folks didn't hear what they were saying on the radio about the race not being close. They said it was about a 30-minute wait and you know the pollster company wanted me at the studio by seven to interview us. But in any event they were having a nice party for all us undecided voters. There are a few really good looking ladies working at the studio so I didn't think it would be smart if I was late.*

*So I didn't actually vote even though I was a "decided voter."*

*Thankfully just like the radio said it didn't make any difference. I know I should have voted and will make sure next time to be "decided" and actually vote.*

*Thanks again for all your help. By the way does anyone know what that Peterson Jury is thinking? As much as I listen to Court TV and Larry King, I can't understand it. It shouldn't take that much time to make up their mind. Well we will see what happens Monday.*

*Sincerely Yours,*

*Clem Kadiddlehopper*

---

## E DAY PLUS SEVEN
## NOVEMBER 9, 2004

Seems like it is more than a week. So many thoughts and concerns:

1. *Maybe it is better for President Bush to have to solve his own problems. Kerry would not know what to do and would face a hostile congress, no money, etc. etc. Bush wants to make major changes and will be aggressive in every area from taxes to Iraq, but will now have to take responsibility for the results.*

2. *There is something very wrong when this controversial and exciting campaign does not get the under 30 crowd out to vote. So many people worked hard on this goal, with little*

*success. It is our children's future, but they don't know it. We are fighting to bring democracy all over the world but our people don't value it.*

3. *The increase in the Latino and Jewish vote for Bush may be an important change in our political landscape. The Blacks are the only minority still completely backing the Democrats.*

4. *Can the nation unite after four years of battles and character assassination? It will be obvious in a month or two if Bush will try. He doesn't have to; and moves to the center will definitely alienate his base. Imagine appointing a Supreme Court judge that supports the current abortion law. Talk about a confirmation battle.*

5. *Hope the military supported Bush. Since they are on the firing line it would be better if they and their families have faith in his judgment. It is hard to die or kill for a cause you do not support. But that is the role of the soldier.*

6. *What happened to the exit polls that were so accurate in some states and wrong in other states? Prepare yourself for years of speculation and conspiracy theories.*

7. *Look for a lot of pressure to have paper trail for electronic voting machines. Too many strange tallies. Again prepare for conspiracy theories of everything from vote counts to registrations.*

8. *Democrats could have easily won, but they continue to lose their traditional base and should go through a soul-searching examination. A lot of decisions have to be made by the party in the next year. We will try to cover these in a few days and welcome your comments.*

9. But the Republicans also have a challenge. The new conservatives are going to demand change in many key areas from deficits to abortion to gay marriage amendment. They may support the President (or maybe a more accurate term is lead the President) but are they a good base for the Republicans to build on. The election brought new problems to both parties.

## KARL, YOU IDIOT. WE WANTED A WIN, BUT YOU TRAPPED ME WITH A MANDATE
## NOVEMBER 21, 2004

We can imagine that this is what Bush is saying these days. Kerry may have lost but Bush is trapped by an ultra-conservative congress that wants to replace Cheney in running the country. Karl Rove did too good a job. He and the country may be the big loser.

Bush was counting on being able to blame the Democrats for not getting anti-abortion judges, cutting more taxes, banning same sex marriage, government regulatory matters, etc., etc. But now he is their prisoner.

You could see the change immediately after the election. Conservatives became very aggressive in TV interviews, speeches, and dictates to the White House. They immediately put Senator Specter in his place. They are out of control even before the new Congress takes office. The Evangelical Christians and business organizations gave generously, worked very hard and now will not take no for an answer.

You don't have to read the demands from Bob Jones University to know that the ultra conservatives are in charge. Yesterday they blocked the Intelligence Reform Bill. They want to protect the Pentagon and want illegal immigration stopped so they have blocked the most important piece of legislation since 9/11. If Bush can't win before the new Congress takes office he can forget about it. It will show that the whole 9/11 Commission was a show.

There is a new boss coming to town in January and his name is not Bush. It will be interesting to see how he tries to control them.

P.S. Many of the Updaters asked if the Update would continue. We will continue to send you our comments on various subjects, but if you want your name off the list, just let us know. No one wants their mailbox filled with unwanted messages.

The Update started as a conversation between a few relatives and it gradually grew. We enjoyed commenting on the election and appreciated your interest, encouragement and participation. It has been fun and we hope informative.

# The End of the Year

**TWO JANUARY ELECTIONS THAT WILL
IMPACT YOUR CHILDREN'S FUTURE
DECEMBER 3, 2004**

## IRAQ.

The US policy is not clear but one thing is for sure, we have to hold the election and try to start the long process of installing a new government. It may not work, but the President does not seem to have any other plan. The question is can the results be legitimate if half the people don't vote? Silly, we just had the same turn out in our country. The election may start a full-scale civil war but the Bush program must proceed if we have any hope of success. We will be in Iraq for a decade, but this election will determine if we will ever be more than an invader who conquered the country.

## PALESTINIAN AUTHORITY

Do they want a moderate, a radical leader or the brilliant leader who is serving life in Prison? Our guess is Barghouti who is sitting in an Israeli prison, will win in a breeze. Talk about a low cost campaign: no travel, no debates, and no tough interviews. If Kerry hears about his he will get arrested before 2008.

Arafat was a genius at attracting world support for his people. The new leader certainly will not be as talented, but he will be the leader who determines continued war or a serious attempt at peace. This election will also determine the future of Israel's current government. Serious peace negotiations will have positive and negative implications for Israel and dramatic impact on our future.

Some Americans find it hard to follow their own election, but these two elections will affect us as much as the Kerry Bush battle in November. Stay tuned.

## RUNAWAY CONGRESS AND COWBOY BUSH
## DECEMBER 4, 2004

This is getting to be interesting. Instead of Bush setting the agenda, Conservatives in Congress are using Rove's campaign tactics against the President. The stupid ads against Kerry now are run by the same people against Bush. We are waiting for the Swift Boat Veterans to Volunteer to Patrol the Rio Grande to stop the illegal immigrants. But if people get excited about "moral values" you can't expect them to support giving drivers licenses to illegal aliens.

The President thinks he got the mandate, but the conservative congress knows better. They gave Bush the mandate and are letting the President know that he can play rough in Iraq, but better behave himself when he is dealing with them.

Well now it is time for Cowboy Bush to mount up and round up these congressmen. Let's see if he can hog tie them and get them to pass the bill or if he has to back down and let them pull the bill apart and wait till next year.

Can you imagine this degree of opposition before the new more conservative congress even starts? And all this over the 9/11 Intelligence Bill, the most advertised and promoted bill in decades. Can't wait till Bush tries to touch the hot rails of social security, judges, draft, etc.

The winner in this battle will give us a good clue as to how the next two years are going to go in Washington. It will be an interesting week.

## LIARS MAY FIGURE,
## BUT ONLY FOOLS BELIEVE
## DECEMBER 8, 2004

Our society is increasingly filled with people who want to manipulate us through false information. Some create government figures on inflation, job creation, unemployment, etc. You have to put this information through the "open eye check."

For example Washington says the inflation figure is less than 3%, but a quick check of my expenses indicates at least a 6% increase. I don't know what the true figure is, but certainly don't want to plan my future on a figure that may be "readjusted" in a year. Business sales are another wild misinformation game. Every Thanksgiving they say everyone is buying and Christmas sales are booming. After January 1st, a couple chains go bankrupt because sales were so bad.

Others like to invent people or events to support their objectives. You might check out the movie "Wag the Dog" for an example of what is going on. Obviously war is filled with misinformation and we need heroes, but stupid lies destroy the honor of our military and make a mockery of real heroes. Private Lynch was a good example. The Pentagon invented a story that no one believed and worse ignored her Sergeant and fellow soldiers who fought heroically.

The latest with former football player Pat Tillman is too stupid to imagine. They made up a story that was immediately exposed as nonsense. Tillman was great American and role model who fought for his country, but the fictitious story of how he fought the enemy dishonors him and his memory. The fact that he was killed by "friendly fire" (a term we never could understand) does not lessen his valor.

Fifty years ago these liars might have gotten away with their stories. But today the Internet communication around the world quickly gets the true story out.

Let's open our eyes, tune in our ears and use our brains. We have to stop the nonsense of people treating us like fools. Our country and our economy will be stronger.


## IT IS BUSH 1 AND THE HOUSE
## CONSERVATIVES 0
## DECEMBER 8, 2004

The President answered the call and beat the opposition on the 9/11 Bill into the ground or at least told them he would deal with their objections next year. Stay tuned. Many battles to come and we will see what happens in this high stake poker game.


## LIGHTENING ROD' RUMSFELD
## IS BURNING OUT
## DECEMBER 18, 2004

It used to be that Don did his job of attracting all the dangerous electricity away from the Pres, but now Bush is holding his hand and conservative jolts are burning both of them.

We were surprised that the Bush Housecleaning, which gave almost his entire cabinet a chance to run before the "you know what hits the fan", would have included Don. After all he has taken a pounding for the last two years and deserves his Medal of Honor and some rest. Our guess is that no one wanted to take over the job, which has as much risk as being the point man on a patrol in Iraq.

Who could have imagined two months ago that Trent Lot and William Kristol would be calling for his resignation? All this because he answered a soldier's question in his usual blunt manner. Well it may go down in history. A National Guard Enlisted man brings down the Defense Secretary. Who could figure?

Our guess is that they believe the war is a lost cause and a successful Iraq election is a long shot, so the Republican supporters of the war want to cover their ass and go on record that the President and his team are not doing a good job. Guess they think it will help in their next election campaign, if the whole venture falls apart.

In any event it is fun to listen to the Conservative Commentators attacking these Republican leaders. They are now getting the "Kerry Treatment." Can't wait to see what happens. Will the Senators back down or will the Commentators jump ship and help them flush Don down the drain?

Bush is getting his introduction to being a Lame Duck President and it is not easy.

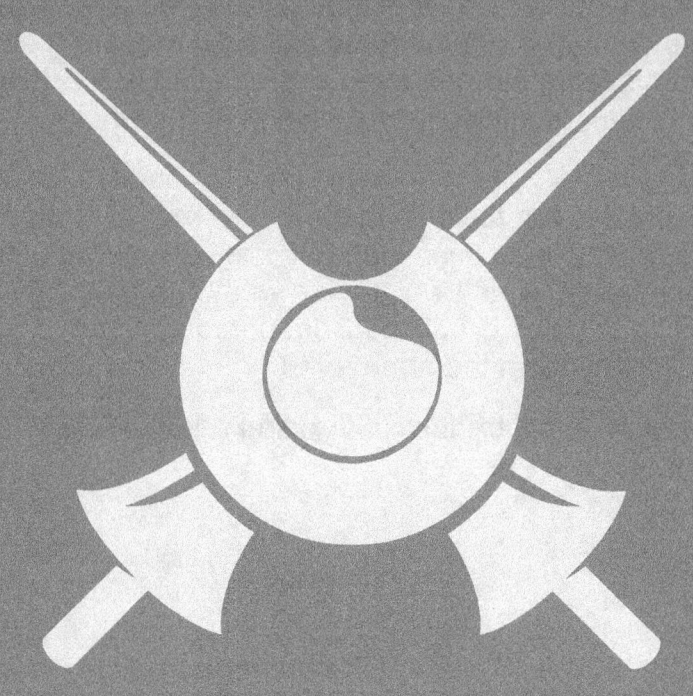

# The New Year

## UPDATE'S NEW YEAR GREETING
## JANUARY 1, 2005

It is tough to talk about a Happy New Year when millions in Asia are suffering and our country is involved in a terrible war in Iraq. Maybe it is more appropriate to give thanks for the food, health and happiness we have enjoyed in 2004 and work to share our blessings with those less fortunate. Best wishes for health and happiness.

## TORTURE A TOUGH SUBJECT
## WITH NO EASY ANSWERS
## JANUARY 9, 2005

The debate in Washington about the Attorney General and our Torture policy is a difficult subject discuss. When a country is invaded whether it is Poland, China or Iraq some citizens resist. The invading army often uses harsh measures to put down the insurgency. The losing army is then tried for War Crimes. Who is a "Patriot" (our term in the Revolutionary War) and who is a "terrorist" depends on which side you are on and which side wins the battle.

As we observed last year, the President's orders have obviously led to torture and no one even knows where many captured insurgents are being held. The Geneva Conventions that we demanded Iraq follow when our soldiers were captured early in the war is now a "quaint" concept. Worse the Pentagon and the Generals who issued these orders are going to Court-Martial a few National Guard Soldiers and hide their own actions.

You can understand both sides of the question but unfortunately you can't have it both ways. Our soldiers are taught to give name, rank and serial number. What we dish out is what our captured soldiers will get in future wars. This is a simple fact but so hard to understand in the midst of the mess we are facing in Iraq.

If we change places with the enemy we might be able to have a clearer picture. This week North Korea (One of the President's Axis of Evil) distributed 33 page booklets with detailed Wartime Guideline on how to behave in the coming war with the U.S.A. Kim Jong II may believe that the coming war is the culmination of 50 years of unsuccessful truce negotiations and the starvation of their people caused by U.S. actions and the money they must spend on defense. This is the situation today, but for the purpose of this discussion let's move to fiction. Let's pretend and change places with the enemy.

Kim Jong II decides to invade the United States before we attack North Korea. He conquers Texas as he blames the Bush Family for the danger to his country and is sure the people of Texas will welcome his troops. The invasion succeeds but the people do not offer flowers and kisses. Kim is surprised that So many Texans have guns and know how to use them. Armed resistance is rampant. North Korea reports that terrorists are coming across the border from Mexico to fight the North Koreans. After many attacks and loses the Koreans get tough and El Paso is flattened by their Army convinced it would break the resistance. Surprisingly the Koreans find that the resistance does not go away but intensifies.

---

Kim Jong Il issues a decree that those insurgents and terrorists who are fighting his army are not entitled to protection of the Geneva Conventions. Torture is authorized to get information to help save the lives of the liberating North Korean Army.

How does this sound? Stupid? Silly? Sensible? You decide. And now back to "Reality" in Washington.


## A HORSE RACE IS ONLY A HORSE RACE UNTIL YOU PLACE YOUR BET! JANUARY 17, 2005

It has taken us time to distill the election and to comment on how both parties have to change in order to win in 2006. We will send these thoughts on for your review in the next few days but first a comment on the new voters.

The most interesting and encouraging thing in our election was that the Republicans brought a lot of new voters to the booth. The Democrats also were successful in this area (but not quite good enough in Ohio). These are not the "Anyone but Bush'" Democrats or 'Let's vote Massachusetts out of the Union" Republicans.

They are new voters and may well switch their vote next time depending on how they feel the Republicans have done for them and the country. In the past they ignored the election (It was just another horse race). But this time they placed a bet and now have a stake in the outcome.

And like a horseplayer, if the horse wins they will bet on the same horse in the next race. If the horse loses, they probably won't.

In addition there were more potential voters, like our friend Clem, who almost made it into the booth but are more interested than before. We will watch to see what Clem and the new voters are thinking as the year progresses. If the economy is strong and the war in Iraq is ending successfully, the Republicans can rest easy as they will get the new Republican voters and a lot of new Democrat voters if not look for a big change in Red and Blue seats in Congress. And that is the way it should be.

Stay tuned for the new Washington dance craze, "The Democrat's Right Step Hop" and "The Republican's Left Step Shuffle."

# THE NEWEST DANCE IN WASHINGTON
# THE DEMOCRAT'S RIGHT STEP HOP!
# JANUARY 18, 2005

**"You take a step to the left, then three to the right one back to the left and you shake it all about. You do the hocus pocus and turn around, that's what it's all about!"**

We wanted to wait till all the For Sale Signs came down in the blue states and the applications for Visas to Canada and Australia were put away before commenting on what the Democrats should do.

They say Jimmy Carter was a weak President but we never saw a weaker President then Bush. Everything was a disaster. The war went from bad to worse. The world thinks he is a joke. If he wasn't using an electronic prompter in the first debate, he should of. Every press conference and meeting had to be staged. We could go on and on. But he won!

We could say Karl Rove ran a tougher and more efficient campaign or that Kerry was a worse candidate than Bush, or that it was the "War President" but the bottom line is the majority of the country rejected the liberal wing of the Democratic Party. For better or worse our country is becoming a land where people have to take care of themselves. If some are weak or uneducated, they will suffer. The country tilted to the right.

In addition many voters were more concerned about gay marriage than about the war in Iraq you have to credit Bush for knowing his constituency. We could go on, but you know the story.

Going to Canada or Australia is not an option and Democrats have to look at themselves in the mirror and decide between three options:

1. *First they could go to the LEFT AND SPLIT. The liberals go one way and the more conservative Democrats go another. Think of a third of the country supporting Dean. If Ralph Nader can influence people with a few votes what could this group do? They are committed and have the brains and money to get their message across. In the past our country has had elections with three or four parties and minority parties can win and /or influence policy. So this is an option but not one we would recommend.*

2. *Or they could go to the RIGHT. Is it better to change the character and traditional values of Party to appeal to more voters? In this scenario, the party promotes moral principles, speaks about religion, takes a hard line on morals etc. etc. It was the Bill Clinton method but they would need a Bill Clinton to carry it off and he is not available. They would lose the liberal wing and need a massive number of Republican voters to change sides in order to have a chance. Not realistic.*

3. *Or they could make a few modifications to the right, stay the course and see where Bush leads. If he has a hard time on Social Security, the war, and tax cuts a few million voters will forget about gay marriage and abortion and start worrying about feeding their family and the war. If Bush leadership proves to be great, the Republicans will continue their coalition and probably win the next election. But remember Kerry ran a weak campaign and still only needed a change in 50,000 voters in Ohio to win the election. We think it makes sense to keep the party intact. Make modifications to the right but no radical changes.*

The Democrats have had devastating defeats in the past remember McGovern, a brilliant legislator and war hero who lost almost every state, yet the party came back. The Democrats should work hard to do the people's business and concentrate on the 2006 Congressional elections where they have many good candidates and tons of issues that favor their traditional position over weak opponents. And don't start the Presidential sweepstakes until the Congressional election is over. So much can happen in three years that it is impossible to know what type of candidate would be right in 2008.

For now Democrats should have fun and do The Right Step Hop.

Who knows the country might start dancing with them.


## CLEM KADIDDLEHOPPER RETURNS! JANUARY 30, 2005

The Update's Number One Non Voter, Comments on the Iraq Election.

---

*Well last fall everyone was picking on me because I had not voted in any election. And I know this was wrong and came very close to voting in November. But I think the election yesterday in Iraq had some lesson for all you "regular" voters.*

*The terrorists said they would kill anyone who voted and a higher percentage of Iraqis voted than in the US. I don't know what that says about our country but maybe they should send some Iraqi election people over to our country to help me and my friends to be more responsible. I was discouraged by a long line at my polling place. If someone said it might be bombed I wouldn't have even thought about voting. A lot of my friends in the suburbs are afraid to go downtown let alone to a possible bombing target.*

*One thing was a little similar. The religious leaders told the people who to vote for and that seems to have been a big thing in our election also. But they had some other things that we might try. Iraq didn't have candidates but rather the people voted for parties. I could have decided to vote Republican or Democrat easier than Bush or Kerry. I think I know where the parties stand but Bush and Kerry confused me no end.*

*Finally things must really be rough in Iraq. If we were in as bad a shape as they am I bet we would get a lot more people voting. So I guess you could say since our country is doing well we don't need guys like me to help to decide on who should be President.*

*Anyway, I just wanted to say that elections sure are interesting and thank you for thinking about me. By the way that Jackson trial is really going to be something. I can't wait for it to start.*

*Sincerely,*

*Clem Kadiddlehopper*

---

# THE REPUBLICAN LEFT STEP SHUFFLE
# JANUARY 31, 2005

"You take a step to the right, three to the left one back to the right and you shake it all about. You do the hocus pocus and you shuffle around that's what it's all about."

We wanted to wait till both parties came down to reality before commenting on how they must change.Last week we suggested what the Democrats should do to win in 2006. They are in a tough situation but it is easier for a party to change after a loss. After all their supporters want to win and realize that things went wrong.

For the Republicans all that talk about a mandate had to be put away and they had to face the need for change if they are going to continue their victory streak. But it is tougher changing after a victory. All their supporters want to see their issues addressed.

First the election brought many ultra conservative congressmen and senators to office. They rode to victory on the story Karl Rove created. Moderate Republicans will have no place in the party and will be candidates to join the Democrats unless the party moves to the left. But if the party does not follow through on the Red State campaign promises they could lose those loyal voters and sow the seeds for a Democratic return in 2006, So George has to move to the left while he placates supporters who are truly worried about moral issues. As an example watch the Left Step Shuffle on Gay Marriage Amendment it should be worth the price of admission.

Next they have to control spending or lose their important and traditional base that believes in fiscal responsibility a painful task with a war going on, slow economy and everyone wanting their reward for bringing out the vote. The President has no excuse for not delivering since Republicans have the White House, both Houses of Congress and you could say the Supreme Court. It will be tough to blame the Democrats for putting our country into huge deficits for years to come.

The President also wants to go down in history as an enlightened leader so he has to again shuffle to the left. His inauguration speech was a study in confusion (They even had to call in his Dad to explain what the President was talking about). Who could argue about liberty for the world? It's the left step shuffle. Certainly many supporters and allies around the world don't want to hear that we are planning to bring liberty to more countries like we have in Iraq. The State of the Union should be much more informative.

There are so many areas that the President has to work on changing philosophy, goals and programs. It is not easy but let's watch the President do the Left Step Shuffle.

## EULOGY TO MAX SCHMELING
## FEBRUARY 4, 2005
## SYMBOLS CHANGE THE WORLD

Events control our lives, but it would be hard to find two more unwitting symbols than Joe Louis and Max Schmeling. After Max beat Joe in their first fight Hitler made Max the symbol of the strength of his Aryan culture and Joe became the champion of black people.

Let us set the stage: The year 1938 and the world and the US were divided. Many in the US wanted to go to war with (not against) Germany. Many in our country believed that Blacks were inferior and in fact were not deemed good enough to be soldiers let alone in any sport that required brains.

So onto this stage in 1938 strode Max and Joe for their rematch. Both good men and both great athletes. The hopes and fears of people around the world were on their shoulders. Hitler demanded a victory from Max and Roosevelt put all his strength and power behind Joe. Jews and Blacks prayed for Joe as a victory would put the lie to Hitler's view about inferior religions and races. It may not have been reasonable but the world was on their back.

The world was glued to their radio sets and the bell sounded. It was over in 2 minutes. Joe demolished Max. Anyone who heard it will remember the fight as if it happened yesterday. It impacted history and possibly our lives today.

After the war Max demonstrated time and again that he was a great man. He didn't ask to be Hitler's champion. Joe didn't ask to our champion.

Today on his death, Max deserves our good thoughts and remembrance.

P.S. Even today we see the remnants of the black athlete controversy. Just last year Rush Limbaugh raised the question about black quarterbacks. Can one win the Super Bowl? Will the question be answered Sunday? Who knows but in most sports the more common question today is where are the white players.

## AL GORE AND HIS LITTLE SOCIAL SECURITY LOCK BOX
## FEBRUARY 8, 2005

Gore tried to make it as simple as he could. He would take the money we pay into the Social Security Fund and instead of spending it on everything else Washington could think of he would put it in a lock box.

George Bush and the late night comics had a ball with Gore's presentation of the problems of Social Security. Well it turns out the joke is on us. Privatizing Social Security may only be a diversion from the much bigger economic problems facing our President and Congress but it is setting the stage for everyone who depends on social security to work longer and get less.

But one solution you will not hear is to put the funds in a lock box. Guess it would make Al Gore look pretty smart.

On a broader view, the social security issue is part of what the voters decided in November. The President expressed his view and the voters endorsed it.

Simply put it is a swing to the right. More individual responsibility and less worrying about those that do not or cannot take care of themselves.

Social Security is just the President's toe in the water. The President believes in making Americans more responsible and independent. Thoughts about being my brother's keeper are being put in the closet. There are benefits to his view. If people take responsibility our country will be stronger. But the downside is if the family cannot respond we will have more hungry and sick kids and more people in prisons if you can imagine the more than the two million people now in prison.

There are many pieces to this goal including medical care, education, affirmative action etc. Social Security is not one of the big problems but it gets the ball rolling. Now we will see if the Red States follow the President. They chose the President and now they will make the difference. It will be interesting to watch.

# The 3-Day Diet

**A LUCKY STRIKE EXTRA FROM
THE POLITICAL UPDATE:
AN EASY TO FOLLOW DIET THAT
COST NOTHING AND SAVES MONEY
FEBRUARY 12, 2005**

We thought we would divert our Update from Politics to another problem facing our society overweight children and adults who are damaging their lives and affecting our country through lost productivity and medical costs.

For decade's dozens of diet plans have taken billions of dollars away from productive investments and our bank accounts. We have been bamboozled, conned, tricked, embarrassed, and just plain fooled into wasting our money. Only a small percent of those who try these diets succeed in the long run, For the vast majority of people, diet plans have not only failed but have delivered mental anguish, embarrassment over failure and damage to health. The problem is simple. We eat too much and we don't eat enough healthy foods.

So let us tell you about a simple diet plan we have been working on for over a year. First there is nothing to buy, no calories or carbs to count, no special foods to cook, no meetings to attend, nothing to read and best of all your friends don't have to know you are on a diet if you don't want to tell them. It is called: Healthy, Half and Hearty—The 3-Day Diet

The plan is simple a three-day rotation of eating styles. Two are basically what you are eating now and the third you know you should be following. Here are all the instructions you need to go on an effective and enjoyable diet:

## THE FIRST DAY IS HEALTHY
You just eat as much healthy food as you like. If you don't know what is healthy, stop reading now as you may have a bigger problem. A healthy day for me would start with grapefruit and oatmeal in the morning, a Turkey sandwich for lunch and some broiled salmon for dinner. You could fill in the vegetables to eat and the doughnuts to avoid. The key is healthy food does not lead to overeating. It is the sugar and high fat content meals that trap us into overeating.

## THE SECOND DAY IS HALF
Normally we eat too much high fat and calorie meals but can easily get by with half the volume and still enjoy the regular diet. On the HALF-DAY you eat your normal meals but only half as much. For me it would mean one doughnut in the morning, going with a friend to McDonalds for lunch and order one super-size combo meal but split it! For dinner order or serve a smaller portion or save half the Spaghetti and Meatballs for dinner the next day. Eat the food you like but don't eat it all. This is not rocket science. You know what "half" means.

## THE THIRD DAY IS HEARTY
This is your reward for following the program on day one and two eat hearty just the way you normally do when you are not on any diet. Here again no special instructions are needed.

Now you are back to day one and ready to start the next three-day weight loss program.

---

The days can be interchanged in your schedule. Let's say you were going to a favorite restaurant or having a special banquet with friends. Just change your day so you can eat Hearty. If you want to eat Hearty two days in a row just follow it up with an extra Healthy or Half.

You can add some bells and whistles if you like. A pin that shows Healthy, Half or Hearty, keep a calendar, give yourself rewards, etc. The key is that 2/3rds off the time you are eating less fattening meals. You will be healthier and happier.

## WHAT A DIFFERENCE A "DAY" MAKES
## FEBRUARY 15, 2005

Remember when we were training and arming Osama Bin Ladin so he could kill Russians in Afghanistan, which by the way he did very well. Now we are berating Russia for not sending troops to help us fight and kill Osama.

Remember when we armed Sadam with WMD's to help him fight the Ayatollahs of Iran. Today Sadam is in prison because we thought he was threatening us with WMD that he didn't have.

Remember when we would do anything to stop Iran from gaining power in Iraq and the Middle East. Well today we are toasting the election (we fought and died for) that will give the power to the Grand Ayatollah and probably convert Iraq into an Islamic country.

Remember when Wal-Mart had a massive advertising campaign telling us how important it was to buy American. Well today they buy 15 billion from China and 50% to 85% of all their merchandise comes from outside the U.S.

Remember when the Democrats indicated that they were going to develop a new image and today Howard Dean is the national chairman.

Remember when we said what a great job our Soldiers were doing in training the Iraqi Army. But today we hear that 72 private companies have been hired to do the job.

We could go on and on in local matters, business or wars. We guess the lesson is that policy by Government or Corporations is designed for today's consumption not tomorrow's or history's review. But there is a side benefit. Every day's newspaper paper offers a lot of humor on the front page. Might as well laugh.

## CLEM GOES ON THE 3H DIET
## FEBRUARY 16, 2005

*It's About Time! You finally are talking about a subject I am interested in. I told you I don't understand politics and your readers don't want to talk about the Jackson Trial (although him being sick sure raises a lot of interesting possibilities) but man do I know about dieting. I have tried every pill and every plan. Some have worked for a while but it was tough and last year's diet was really expensive eating steaks every night.*

*Well my girlfriend is complaining that I have a potbelly and your 3H plan arrived just in time. I started it today eating hearty of course and am trying to decide whether to go healthy or half tomorrow. Either way I really loaded up today that should carry me through tomorrow without any problem.*

*I do have a question. Would a plain triple hamburger and sour cream baked potato be healthy? I usually get the Wendy Bacon Burger and fries so it would be quite an improvement. Let me know as soon as possible.*

*Possibly you could publish a list of how to follow the 3H Diet at McDonalds. I have been looking at their menu and it isn't easy. A list like that would help a lot of your readers.*

*Anyway I am weighing in at 189 and hope to knock off at least 10 pounds any idea how long this will take? Will keep you informed on my progress.*

*Sincerely yours,*

*Clem Kadiddlehopper*

*P.S. Still would like to hear about what you think about the Jackson case. He is weird but so are the doctors that put him in the pediatric ward in the hospital. Boy I wish I could be on that Jury.*

---

## PRESIDENTS DAY, VOTING DAY AND PAROLE DAY ALL IN THE NEWS TODAY
## PRESIDENT'S DAY 2005

Senators Hillary Clinton and John Kerry are proposing that Voting Day become a national holiday. The Republicans will no doubt scuttle this issue, as they believe most of the people unable to find time to vote are Democrats. And you can make a good argument that it may not be wise to try to convince half of the country to vote. If they do not care who their elected leaders are, maybe they should be left alone.

But on the other hand today we are celebrating President's Day and the chances are you have not heard one remembrance of our past Presidents. In fact it is just another holiday for government workers and no mail. So maybe trading a President's Day for a Voting Day every year or two might be worth a try.

---

The second proposal by Clinton and Kerry is much more critical. Ex-convicts have lost their right to vote in many states. With over two million people in prison and tens of thousands being released every year do we really want to exclude these people from their role in society and the right to choose their leaders? Remember anyone can end up in prison a few bad checks, bad accident, smoking the wrong cigarettes, etc., etc. How would you feel losing your right to vote after you paid your so-called debt to society?

Our democracy can and has survived indifference on the part of many voters, but will not long endure the exclusion on those who want to vote. We have seen the result of this in both our country and around the world. Democracy does not survive in a vacuum.

## THE ELECTION CONNECTION
## FEBRUARY 27, 2005

Many elections on the local, national or international stage are not very honest. The party in power molds the rules to fit their candidate. But the charges about crooked elections have a long life.

Mayor Daley's Chicago vote for John Kennedy was notorious. We still hear commentators talking about the vote and it possibly even contributed to the hatred that led to his assassination.

The Florida vote for George Bush is much more famous as the world could see the whole battle played out on television. And the controversy affects our lives today.

The election in Iraq may have been a great success. But charges abound about the honesty of the count. It seemed obvious that the Shiites would win and have massive power in forming the constitution and in turn the official leaders next year. Anyone with half a mind knows that this is not acceptable to our Government and you can only imagine what stories will come out in the next year as the results are implemented.

Russia was making good progress in building democracy when Putin took a big step back. George Bush just completed a trip to bring Putin back in line. Unfortunately Putin brought up Bush's election in 2000 and that his father's Supreme Court put Bush in office and hence he should not be lecturing anyone about honest elections. The President backed down as you would when faced with this comment. Of course he could have said that no one poisoned Gore but the discussion was not going anywhere.

Election problems have a long life. We will hear much more about the count in Iraq, Moscow and Florida and probably still more about Chicago.

## THE TALE OF TWO WAGES
## MARCH 8, 2005

Two stories were in the news today. They may seem to be miles apart but in effect are closely related and a key to the future of our democracy.

The first story was about the 2004 compensation of some executives. James Cayne the CEO of Bear Stearns was paid 24.7 million plus another 6.5 million of interest on deferred compensation stocks. That's about $15,000 an hour. Of course not every executive did that well. The co-presidents under Cayne only made about 24 million. And others really had a rough year like Jeffrey Immelt of GE whose total compensation was only around 17 million. These obviously are big jobs.

The second story was that congress voted down (twice) an increase in the minimum wage $5.15 an hour. This must obviously be for small jobs.

We as a country are promoting democracy and capitalism all over the world. Stories like this make the job very difficult. You decide. Is this a story that promotes our way of life or threatens our way of life?

One note: Many European countries have standards and limits on what the president of a corporation can earn in comparison to the wages of the lowest paid worker in their corporation. We would tell you this figure but don't want Mr. Cayne to feel bad.

But you can imagine it is much less than 3,000 times - the difference between Mr. Cayne's salary and the wage that Congress thinks is adequate for someone else.

## CLEM REPORTS ON THE 3H DIET
## MARCH 19, 2005

*I want to give you a report on the 3H Diet. But first I want to thank the Updaters for their suggestions especially two people who answered my call for advice on how to eat healthy at McDonalds. You have a very friendly group. Especially when they are not talking about politics.*

*Ceci in the Florida Sun wrote: Clem: How tall are you? At 189 pounds you have some meat on your bones. Lift weights and you'll look sexy.*

*If you want to eat at McDonald's get the grilled chicken sandwich. If you want a salad, eat at Wendy's because their salads are better.*

*Thanks Ceci, I am almost 6 feet. The Chicken is good, but I am loyal to McDonalds and will have to think about changing my dining habits and going to Wendy's*

*Marsha on the Oregon Trail wrote: You asked for suggestions on how to follow the 3H diet at McDonalds. Of course, it'll take a little longer to knock off 10 pounds eating at McDonalds this way.*

*Day 1 - Healthy - Sorry, Clem, no McDonald's on healthy days. That's the safest way to avoid temptation. If you can't stay away, try a side salad with Low-Fat Dressing. No French-fries for dessert!*

*Day 2 - Half - Try a Hamburger Kids Meal. You get all the McDonald tastes you love, in a small serving size. Best of all - you'll love the toys you get!!*

*Day 3 - Hearty - Get a meal deal and Super-Size it!! If you want to shed your pounds a little faster - just get a regular meal deal - leave the supersize for someone else.*

*Lots of luck with your diet, Clem!*

*Marsha's ideas were OK but I had a hard time getting the Kids Meals and then they didn't want to give me the toy. I threatened to boycott them for a day but they would not give in. The Kids Meal was good but I was hungry.*

*OK here is my report. Actually the 3H Diet isn't bad but I am not losing much weight. Down only 4 pounds. The Hearty part is easy and the Half is working ok because I go to those places where they serve all you can eat and only eat half of what I normally do. But the Healthy is rough. I look at the menu and don't like any of the things that you might consider healthy. End up with a salad that I don't even finish.*

*Anyway my girlfriend is happy that I am on your diet and she might try it too. That would make it easier for the Half days where we could split the SuperSize Meals. Thanks for the encouragement. By the way, the trials in California are sure exciting. The guilty movie stars get off free but that MJ is really sick. Wish I could be on the jury.*

# TALK ABOUT WHACKING A HORNETS NEST
# MARCH 31, 2005

We did not want to comment on the ordeal of Terri Schiavo while she was still alive. It is a tragedy for her and now the family will live with this issue for many more years. The case has challenged our beliefs and our religion. It truly was a hornet's nest of emotions and beliefs.

Let's take a few minutes to review what happened.

After the November election we discussed the tightrope the President and Republican Congress would have to walk with the right wing conservative voters. They delivered the election for Bush and now wanted their beliefs supported. Congress did not deal with their key issues like Gay Marriage Amendment or confirming anti-abortion judges so they thought Terri Schiavo would be a clever diversion and further divide the country against the Democrats. They hammed up their concern with a lot of nonsense and more or less said, "Let Them Save Terri." You might compare it to what Marie Antoinette supposedly said to the hungry "Let Them Eat Cake."

Well the hornets didn't just sting the Democrats they swarmed around the hypocrisy of the President, Congress, Gov. Jeb Bush, dozens of judges, etc. Right to life has become a much bigger issue. Simply put, thou shall not kill. This goes beyond the thousands of people like Terri, (whether or not they have a living will); way beyond abortion to dozens of ways most people die and include executions and war.

For the President, (a former governor of a state that annually executes more inmates than most of the world) could soon be considered to be the equivalent of being the biggest abortionist. Both may be legal but both are immoral in the eyes of many religious leaders. The public may demand a much wider litmus test for judges.

The Terry Shiva case has brought diverse leaders from the Pope to Jesse Jackson to state their long held belief that all life is to be preserved.

The Republican and Democratic politicians that supported intervention in state law whacked the hornet's nest and now will be running for their life to avoid being stung. Judges and the Schiavo family are the first people in physical jeopardy but it will go way beyond them. It is easier to start major moral and religious debates than it is to end them. Our experience in the Middle East should make this obvious.

"Let them eat cake" may have ignited the French revolution. Let Them Save Terri, may have ignited a moral revolution in our country.

We welcome your thoughts and comments.


## FIRST, TELL ME THAT YOU LOVE ME
## APRIL 14, 2005

Our country loves to be lied to. No matter how many events unfold as lies we still want to believe that our government always tells us the truth. We love patriotic slogans and nonsense that would embarrass a recruiting Sergeant.

Every day the papers are filled with stories that can't possibly be true. For example the Administration keeps talking about when we will withdraw from Iraq. In fact if we do withdraw it will make the whole war even more ridiculous.

Congress is searching for the so-called "breakdown in intelligence" that lead to our invasion while they fall for the same nonsense about us withdrawing. Most people realize it is propaganda and our intelligence is excellent, but we still like to be told fairy tales.

Also the paper tells the story of the Cuban who blew up a Cuban Passenger Plane killing 73 passengers and tried to kill Castro. We got him out of jail in Panama and now lo and behold he turns up in Florida. We say we hate terrorists and must stop them at any cost. But promote and protect "our terrorists" all around the world

You could go on and on. Politicians attacking Tom DeLay when only a few of them could survive a close scrutiny of their own activities.

The answer must be that we love being told blatant lies even if we know what is going to happen next.

Or who knows, maybe as Colonel Jessup says in "A Few Good Men" we just can't handle the truth!

## WHILE WE ARE WAITING FOR THE WHITE SMOKE MAYBE WE SHOULD REVIEW THE VATICAN'S ELECTION PROCESS APRIL 18, 2005

The Pope is one of the most important leaders in the world and usually has a longer term of office than leaders such as our Presidents. The Vatican has a lot of experience in electing Popes, so maybe we should compare their electoral system with ours and see which makes more sense.

Intelligent Electorate: Not every Catholic can vote only 115 Cardinals who are knowledgeable and very interested in the future of their Church. Looks like they win here. We have a difficult time getting voters interested. In some recent village elections only 20 percent of the eligible voters voted. Not really a democracy.

Even in our recent hotly contested Presidential election probably no more that 40 percent of the eligible voters even bother to register and then half of them do not vote. And with all due respect to our friend Mr. Kadiddlehopper, does it make sense to work so hard to get a person like Clem to participate. No the Vatican wins on having the thinking people select their leader.

Speed: Half of our time is spent preparing for the next election and then the other half is spent arguing about the results. Think of what we could do if we could lock a select group of leaders (maybe the Governors and the Senators) in a room for a few days and out comes our new President. Talk about productivity!

Cost: We could go a long way toward ending poverty in the country by diverting all the money spent by the government and the candidates in every election.

Support: After the election we would not have big arguments in the Senate because, they choose the President. It should make things more productive.

Fraud: We sort of hate to bring this up but the Vatican has handled this well for centuries. Each Cardinal brings his ballot up one at a time (compare this to Florida in 2000) then the ballots are sewn together and then counted. No double voting, no chads and no funny business.

Smoke Signal: Our politicians are really good at blowing smoke, so I guess this is a tie.

Finally, and I hate to bring this up, but could the Vatican Election Process possibly bring us a worse President than we seem to elect with our complicated system of campaigning, financing, primaries, debates, etc., etc., etc.

Well our congratulations and best wishes to the new Pope and to the electoral process that selected him.

## BUSH IN THE RUMBLE SEAT
## APRIL 24, 2005

After the election it seemed that the President was driving a powerful racing car and going to get his real agenda moving forward. He intended to ignore all the phony issues that Karl Rove used in the campaign such as illegal immigrants, liberal judges, worthless UN, etc. etc. and focus on the critical issues facing the country such as the budget, Iraq, social security, etc.,

Unfortunately for him and the country some of his supporters are still in the campaign mode and are focusing on fulfilling his promises whether he likes it or not. They moved Bush out of the driver's seat and put him in the rumble seat where he is just along for the ride.

Hence they pushed John Bolton for the UN, talk about closing the borders, use the nuclear option to get the conservative judges approved, etc. etc. The new drivers are Tom Delay who is fighting for his survival by focusing the spotlight on major diversions such as Teri Schiavo and Bill Fisk who thinks he could take over the religious conservative vote to win nomination in 2008.

Well Bush is going to have to get back in the driver's seat if he doesn't want his presidency to go down the drain. Our guess is Bush will distance himself from their ranting and raving and in effect throw Tom and Bill out of the car.

First Bolton probably won't be approved and if so will be damaged merchandise (think of Justice Clarence Thomas). Then powerful Republicans will tell Tom it is time to fess up on the kickbacks and look for a new career.

Finally they will then let Bill fail in getting the Senate voting rules changed which will lose him the religious conservatives and thus his presidential strategy. Nice part about that is it will make Jeb Bush the leading candidate which George should like after all Jeb elected George in 2000 and a family has to stick together.

---

Talk about a fast race.

It is amazing. The Democrats in complete disarray will do nothing and come out looking like patriots and statesmen. Who could figure?

Cost: We could go a long way toward ending poverty in the country by diverting all the money spent by the government and the candidates in every election.

Support: After the election we would not have big arguments in the Senate because, they choose the President. It should make things more productive.


## MINUTEMEN, JUDGES AND BEARS OH NO! APRIL 27, 2005

It's fun time in Washington again.

As we discussed in the last Update, the Conservative Republicans who went all out to elect the President now want their views implemented and you might say their pound of flesh. Frankly, we can't blame them. If we had worked hard to elect a President and then saw him reneging on the issues we were concerned with, we would be upset too.

The President is trying to placate them with a smoke screen of tough talk but no action. These groups are not buying it. They are taking action on their own in many areas. The Minutemen who are growing by leaps and bounds are ready to defend our border from the "Mexican Invasion." This is a reaction to the driver's license hysteria that was promoted during the campaign. The illegal border crossing has been going on for decades and our economy depends on this labor force so what is a President and former governor of Texas supposed to do.

Obviously the President can't allow the Minutemen to continue this action without a serious incident occurring. But they are armed and dangerous probably more so to Washington than the illegals but they are a growing force.

The judges are another powder keg. If the Republicans do not pass the "nuclear option", they will infuriate their religious conservatives who are counting on the President appointing at least two conservative Supreme Court justices that will overthrow Roe vs. Wade. And make no mistake; this is all about the Supreme Court overturning the historic 1973 decision that legalized abortions.

The bears (fiscal conservatives) are concerned about the wild spending and gigantic deficit. But the Republican Congress that has not pleased their conservative constituents with legislation, want to at least bring home some "pork." You know five or ten million going to a small town can make a guy much happier even if the abortion clinic is still in town.

Best of all, right wing radio (who also sincerely believes they elected the President) are in full attack mode to whip up support for the Minutemen, judges and spending.

This will come to a powerful conclusion soon. The president has to stop them and then the Minutemen might start patrolling Washington, the party will attack Frisk and the conservatives will cut the budget.

Oh well you have to feel sorry for George. There is a price to pay even if you are President.

## THE 30TH ANNIVERSARY OF THE FALL OF SAIGON. CAN ANYONE TELL US WHY OR WHY NOT?
## APRIL 28, 2005

As we commemorate the ending of the Viet Nam war, the papers, radio and TV are filled with a review of the war and the horrendous affect on the Vietnamese people and of course our military forces. The loss of life, wounded people, cities destroyed, Agent Orange effect on friend and foe alike, economy, divisive civil strife, etc., is simply staggering.

Frankly, it is too much pain for most of us to understand or contemplate

It would be easier to accept and understand if anyone could tell us why this war was in our national interest and/or how it has helped our position in the world.

If no one can make sense out of the war or at least explain our policy that too should be taught in our schools. One way or another our children have the right to learn from history.


## IT LOOKS LIKE ANOTHER SLAM DUNK!
## APRIL 30, 2005

Just found out George Tenet's new position in the administration advising the President on Social Security.

Well, talk about going from the frying pan into the fire. The private accounts plan is dead. It frightened too many people. Of course it didn't help that the Stock Market was tanking while the President was selling his plan.

But now the idea where the middle class and upper class will lose benefits while the poor continue to get their benefits is right up there with the advice about finding WMD in Iraq. Sounds like a

Tenet Slam Dunk to us and the President is jumping into the fire.

Seriously, George Bush is taking a beating on so many fronts that he better get a new advisor on domestic affairs. The red states may love the President, but they love their Social Security much more. Someone will have to tell them about "guns or butter" or today you could call it "Sadam or retirement."

In the meantime the Democrats are having a field day but soon will have to discuss their ideas, which may make an equal number of people angry.

## THANK HEAVENS; THE PEOPLE WHO TORTURED IRAQI PRISONERS ARE BEING PUNISHED.
## MAY 2, 2005

It took a while but the President and Pentagon spared no effort to make it clear that we believe in the Geneva Conventions and the ringleaders will pay the price. As we wrote last August (attached), we expected that the Pentagon would find the ringleaders and they would not be in Washington or in the Pentagon, and we were right.

One of the most apprehensible torturers, Pfc. Lynndie England, an Army Reserve records clerk from Maryland, diabolically planned and implemented the systematic torture from Guantanamo to Abu Ghraib. She was going to make some stupid defense about being innocent but she saw what happened to her other high level conspirator, Pvt. Graner, who would not plead guilty and was sentenced to 10 years. But it doesn't end there (for those of you who are "doubters"); responsibility goes all the way up to the top National Guard General Karpinski is expected to get a "letter of reprimand" in her file.

Thank you Secretary of Defense Don Rumsfeld for your fearless leadership. You have calmed the concerns of our Military who fear they may someday be a POW counting on the Geneva Conventions to protect them and the world that was concerned about our morals.

## WHAT COULD BE WORSE THAN NOT CAPTURING OSAMA ? WHY CAPTURING HIM OF COURSE!
## MAY 12, 2005

From all reports we are zeroing in on Osama Bin Laden. Two years ago the Update suggested that he was in the only place in the world where we could not look his home in Saudi Arabia. However, we hope that the reports are accurate and we will soon track him down but and this is a big BUT we must kill him.

Many newspaper and magazine articles have been written about the problems we have with prisoners. Sooner or later they must be put on trial or released. Some may never be heard from but enough are getting out with their story of confinement. If they continue to document abuse it could be much more devastating than the stories we have had up to date.

On the other hand trials are difficult and that is why we haven't had any.

 It is obvious we don't know what to do with a top prisoner like Sadam Hussein. The first legal hearing we tried was a disaster and a full trial now with representation by top U.S. Lawyers will be exciting to watch but not a victory for the new Iraqi Government and our country no matter what the outcome.

A trail for Osama would be 10 times worse than Sadam. He is a hero to millions and it would be hard imagine a trial in the U.S. or Iraq. So let's hope that we find where he is hiding and remember that killing Osama is the goal capturing him is the disaster.

## MISSION ACCOMPLISHED
## BECOMES MISSION IGNORED
## MAY 15, 2005

Don't believe the President really wanted our country to think the war was over when he put up that banner on the Aircraft Carrier; however, it seems to have worked out that way. No matter how bad the situation is in Iraq, most of us are very happy to pretend that we won the war now want to get on to the critical subjects facing our country you know things like the runaway bride and the senseless killing of two little girls in Illinois.

Forget that we invaded Iraq and have been unable to maintain order (the responsibility of the invading country) a failure of our military but more accurately our policy makers who did not and have not sent in enough troops to do the job and now are befuddled by the entire matter.

We are creating a market for suicide bombers to sacrifice their life and attack our presence in Iraq. Don't see how they will quit when they are so successful. They are killing an average of 6 victims (and wounding many more) for each bomber. No one knows as every news account is filled with terms like "at least 8 civilians killed" or "more than 20 police wounded" and there is no follow up. Any army would love those odds so the bombers are wining. They are intelligent and many from the wealthy families of Saudi Arabia (you remember them don't you the guys that attacked us on 9/11). The bombers won't run out of bombs so we are in a dilemma.

We aren't losing many soldiers, but Iraqi military and plain people are being slaughtered every day. Many people in our country don't want to think about the war (other than heroically putting up "We Support Our Troops" sticker on their SUV) and certainly don't get emotional about the dead, wounded and orphaned children who are the victims of these bombs and the war.

Maybe it is too overpowering for most of us to realize that we bear the responsibility for their death and misery. Who knows we might have to even start listening to the real news again.

## LIKE IT OR NOT BOLTON IS THE RIGHT MAN TO REPRESENT OUR PRESIDENT
## MAY 17, 2005

The Vice President and his associate the President have strong feelings about the UN. It goes back decades. They don't like it, don't believe in it and above all do not want to be subordinate to other countries in any way.

It is just like Social Security, they feel the country under Roosevelt made a mistake and it is up to them to make the people to be responsible for their own financial security. The concept of taxing some for the needs of others upsets them. These are their sincere views.

We have seen billboards attacking the UN and many Republicans making fun of it for forty years so why in the world would we expect George Bush to nominate a supporter of the UN to represent his administration. John Bolton will be honest, direct and represent the Vice President and the President. At least he will not be confused like Colin Powell when he had to lie to get our policy across.

Like it or not we elected George to two terms as President. His views were well known. So why be surprised. I guess you can call it democracy in action. If Bolton wins (and we think he will) it should make Republicans and Democrats happy. The Republicans because they got their man in the UN and the Democrats because the country will see the President's man in the UN.

## WELL HERE WE GO READING THE HEARTS AND MINDS OF POLITICIANS AGAIN
## MAY 27, 2005

We may be premature (and we have been known to be so) but it seems that the fourteen Senators are patriots banding together to save the country from the current civil war that is being promoted by the administration and the leaders of both parties. The country has huge problems and nothing worthwhile is getting done.

The Gang of Fourteen has in effect started a third party. Nothing can get done without these Senators if they stick together. Any sensible idea will get their support and pass. Dangerous and stupid ideas from either party will fail. Suddenly the term Advise and Consent means something. The President has to deal with them and in effect they are saying: "Cut the shit or we will cut it out for you."

Now here is where the plot gets exciting. Who is the titular head of the third party our old Naval Hero John McCain? He is the sugar that attracts the seven Republicans and the glue that has earned the seven Democrat's trust. So let's dig a little deeper.


## REVENGE OF THE BOMBER

 John McCain thought he was on his way to the Republican Nomination (and the Presidency) in 2000 when Karl Rove turned his dogs lose. The Bush attack did an amazing job converting the Naval Hero into a coward. (In case you missed the show in 2000 I am sure you caught the rerun last year staring John Kerry.) You know a few negative facts played up to sound like the hero was really Benedict Arnold.

At the time McCain had every reason to believe he would win the nomination and the Presidency after all his opponent had little going for him except the Bush name. And of course Bush and

Cheney made a career out of avoiding the war in Viet Nam.

Well the deed was done and McCain lost his chance to run the country. But like all warriors if they are not dead they are planning the next battle and Senator McCain smiled and smiled and waited and waited for five years until now. This week he attacked with deadly effectiveness. If his fourteen rebels stay together he will have a lot to say about the war, the Pentagon, Social Security, Stem Cells, taxes, etc, etc, etc.

The timing of the attack was amazing a crucial time in the history of the Congress. The Memorial Day weekend honoring those who fought plus a new movie telling the story of Naval Pilot John McCain and his five years at the Hanoi Hilton (Viet Nam Prison). We can expect Karl Rove and his media army to attack McCain, but it won't be easy as this time the old Naval Pilot is armed and dangerous. This time if they play rough with him, they may be the one who gets hurt.

Maybe the coalition will fall apart. But we believe these Senators are ready to risk everything in order to stop the civil war and move the country forward.

It is historic. It is amazing. And our descendants may be studying it for decades.

# IMPEACHMENT IN THE AIR
## JUNE 18, 2005

We have been waiting for the "I" word and this week the airways were filled with the call to arms.

The liberals are using the Downing Street Memos as proof that the President lied from the beginning about Iraq and want to start Impeachment action. After all they say if Clinton was impeached for sex why Bush shouldn't be impeached for causing over a hundred thousand people dying in Iraq and putting our Army in a Viet Nam scenario. If you need the "facts" listen to Air America (In Chicago 850 on your AM dial).

But not to be left behind in the Impeachment game the conservatives are calling for Sen. Durbin of Illinois to be impeached for his repeating what a FBI agent reported about the torture going on in Guantanamo and then comparing it to murderous regimes. They say he is a traitor. If you need the "facts" on this impeachable offense listen to the conservative "media stars", Rush or Hannity (in Chicago 890 on your AM dial).

In fact the best comedy show in town is to switch back and forth between these two radio stations. Air America is filled with relentless attacks on the Bush Administration while right wing radio is promoting Bush for Sainthood. It is hilarious and free.

But if you are a serious political junkie you should only listen to the "other" side. If you wear Red only listen to Air America and practice your arguments. If you wear Blue, listen only to Rush and Hannity and their want-a-be's. It is educational and if you can beat the other side's arguments (in your mind), you can relax knowing that your views are correct.

P.S. These radio programs make a difference. Newsweek observed last week that if Watergate had happened this year, Rush, Hannity and the powerful conservative radio would have beaten the Washington Post into pieces and Nixon would not have resigned and left office as a hero at the end of his term.

---

# CLEM RETURNS TO THE UPDATE
# JUNE 19, 2005

We thought we lost him, but Clem returns to the Update and comments on National Issues. As you may remember Clem Kadiddlehopper was the Undecided voter that we followed in the last election. He ended up planning to vote for Bush and seemed to get much more interested in politics. Since his views are so important we are reproducing his email message.

---

*Hi Updaters:*

*Well just as many of us thought, those California Juries are nuts. How could they find Jackson not guilty on so many things that all of us knew he was guilty of? Boy I wish I had been on the Jury, you can be sure it would be a different verdict. Oh well, I think the problem was the Mother who let her son "play" with Michael around my neighborhood, the parents check out the "play dates" more seriously.*

*Anyway, the reason I am writing is that I just read yesterday's Update and it brought me back to the international situation. Frankly it was more fun following the Jackson trial, but I was surprised at how bad the war in Iraq has gone while I was concentrating on the trial. The President was on the air yesterday saying how we have to tough it out, when I thought after the election in Iraq and all the celebrating in Washington that those terrorists would have given up. Frankly I am disappointed and a little concerned.*

*Another problem I have with the President is this Social Security thing. I don't want it to change. It has been good for my Mother and otherwise you know who would have to get a second job and support her or worse move her in with me and my girlfriend, a situation that would be difficult to say the least.*

*Finally, and this is of course personal, but I have strong feelings that abortion should be allowed and wonder why everyone is talking about having the Supreme Court outlaw it. Seems to me they have more important things to worry about.*

*So all in all both the California legal system and the Washington leaders need some help. Let me know what you think about Jackson getting off and whether you think he can get his career going again. It sure is interesting.*

*Sincerely yours,*

*Clem Kadiddlehopper*

---

# All "Roves" Lead to the White House

## ALL "ROVES" LEAD TO THE WHITE HOUSE
## JULY 6, 2005

We were hoping to resist discussing the Valerie Plame case, as so much has been written about it. But there are a few comments that we cannot resist.

1. *It is a serious charge. Let's say you were the wife of a Pakistan diplomat that used to work out in the same health club as Valerie and once in a while had lunch or coffee together. By now you and your husband would be back in Pakistan hoping to save your life. Being in contact with a ratted out CIA Undercover Agent is not conducive to good health, whether or not any espionage was going on.*

2. *The columnists who are going to jail are not doing it for journalistic freedom, they are afraid of telling all they know. A few months in jail is much safer.*

3. *The story goes right to the White House. The resigned press secretary or Karl Rove is the beginning of the story, not the end. Someone fed them the secrets and gave them permission to leak the information.*

4. *Our old classmate Robert Novak is ending his illustrious career on a sour note. His program, The Capital Gang, has been taken off the air in anticipation of his confession. He says he will tell all when it is "over" a theory that has its roots in the theory, "the first liar does not have a chance"*

5. *If you are from Illinois you know Patrick Fitzgerald will not be deterred by political influences. Our former Governor (Republican) and Mayor (Democrat) will tell you that he could care less if you are guilty watch out.*

6. *There is a new head of the CIA but most of the top management is the same. They want revenge for politicians playing politics with their lives. After all they just finished falling on their sword for the White House by taking the blame for inaccurate intelligence in Iraq.*

It is another amazing story coming out of Washington. Better than a mystery novel.


## WE REGRET GOING TO THE DARK SIDE BUT IT IS IMPORTANT TO LEARN FROM THE PAST. LET'S CALL IT: THE LAW OF UNINTENDED CONSEQUENCES
## JULY 10, 2005

As we face the national dilemma of fighting al Qaeda around the world, it is wise to remember where they came from.

 We helped create, arm and finance al Qaeda to bring their jihad to Afghanistan to drive the Russians out. The U.S. even named the movement "al Qaeda" came from the U.S. computer file on Osama's operatives. They were our allies. Osama was the leader we picked to do the job. He was wealthy (over 300 million and the ability to borrow from his family), educated, totally committed and ruthless.

It took years of horrible battles but in 1968 the Russians had enough bloodshed, admitted defeat and left Osama and the Taliban in charge. Al Qaeda turned the country into a training camp for new members and we all know the rest of the story.

Unintended Consequences.

## BUSH AND THE SENATE LOOK FOR NOVEL WAY TO AVOID SUPREME COURT CONTROVERSY JULY 12, 2005

If the President picks a judge who is against abortion the right is happy and the left goes on the attack. If he picks a conservative judge that is not against abortion, the left is happy and right goes on the attack. He can't win with either scenario. He desperately has the keep the country together or loses the focus on the war and destroys what is left of his leadership ability.

And it may be fantasy but an alternate ending in the air.

Alternate ending number one, Chief Justice Rhenquist resigns and then talks Sandra Day O'Connor to stay on for a year or so as Chief Justice appoint a conservative to replace Rehnquist and the court remains basically the same. This would require a little conspiracy between O'Connor and Rehnquist but since they used to date in college it is not impossible.

Alternate ending number two is that the President appoints a Republican Senator to the Supreme Court. No record of how he would judge on any issue because he never has been a judge. And no matter whom he selects, the Senate would confirm him or her very quickly after all they are club members.

Possible or not, it is interesting and we love it. Anton Chekhov would have a ball.

## SCORE ONE FOR BUSH AND ONE LOSS FOR THE SUPREME COURT
## JULY 20, 2005

We are sad that the selection had to be based in the candidate's lack of exposure to the abortion issue, but Bush didn't have much choice. Roberts is enough of a Washington insider that the Democrats can't attack him successfully. Doubt if the "Gang of 14" will go to the mat over this candidate. They have to pick their battle carefully.

So the Democrats will have a two-month party and attack Roberts and the Republicans on abortion and human rights in the hope of winning votes in the next election and of making the next justice nomination even more difficult for Bush. In the end he will be confirmed.

It would have been better if Bush could have picked the best person for the job, other than a safe choice about abortion. But this is our country.

P.S. In the meantime our Update on "All Roves Lead to the White House" seems to be on target. Someone has to fall on their sword in a hurry or Bush will have a big problem.

## CLEM GIVES DIET UPDATE
## JULY 20, 2005

*Well, you had a good idea on the "Healthy, Half and Hearty Diet" but the bottom line is I am not losing much. Actually today I am down to 185, about 4 pounds less than when I started. Helen, my girlfriend, says that at least I stopped gaining weight so she is not as upset as I am.*

*Your diet is pretty good, but I am having a hard time following the rules. For example you said if I want to change a Half Day for a Hearty Day (for any special reason) it was ok as long as I kept track and caught up. Well I have keep track but now I am 41 Half Days behind!*

*The Healthy Day is a little easier as I usually order a salad at McDonalds and it is pretty bad so I just suffer and get through it. Another Healthy Day that works is the Double Big Mac without the bread. It is not bad as long as you get the French Fries and I sure feel healthy when I order it at the counter. They are starting to call me "Mr. Diet Man."*

*The other problem is after a Healthy Day I really eat a lot the next day probably something psychological. Anyway Helen is on the diet too and she is doing better maybe you should use her as one of those "testimonials" instead of me. But she doesn't want anyone to know her weight so I don't know if that would work.*

*To get back to the political scene, I am really sorry I planned to vote for President Bush. We don't like the Supreme Court outlawing Abortions. Seems to me he has enough problems to worry about in Iraq and could leave us alone. Bet if his daughter got pregnant tomorrow, she would be first in line at the clinic. Anyway I don't plan to vote for him next time that is if I decide to vote.*

*Keep them Updates coming? Some of them are good.*

*Sincerely yours,*

*Clem Kadiddlehopper*

## YOU CAN HEAR THE QUACKING!
## JULY 31, 2005

The decision of Senator Frist to support Embryonic Stem Cell Research is a dramatic example that George Bush has become a "Lame Duck" President.

The war is a disaster that is getting harder and harder to sell. The Karl Rove story has the potential to devastate the White House. His Social Security initiate is a lost cause. His budget has become an anchor around the conservative members of congress. The result is declining influence over his party.

No doubt Bill Frist sincerely believes in Stem Cell Research (especially with his family founding Hospital Corporation of America), but two months ago he would not have taken on the President. Today he believes the conservative voting block will weaken in the next two years and is broadening his base to run for the Presidency, so he will vote his conscience rather than walk the plank with the President.

Baring some major success in Iraq, the President is going to have less and less influence in his party and with the voters who put him in office.


## WELL, HERE WE GO AGAIN
## BACK TO THE DARK SIDE
## AUGUST 6, 2005

Today is the 60th Anniversary of the first nuclear bomb. Hiroshima suffered 160,000 dead. Right or wrong it changed the world and now our enemies, especially the ones who do not represent a country where we could retaliate, consider using atomic or hydrogen bombs fair game.

Now let's review our current concern. We know Osama wants to get a nuke so he can attack a U.S. City and their latest video message talks about killing thousands of Americans.

We are negotiating to stop North Korea from building a few bombs and Iran from getting started. This is good but Russian has 17,000 bombs and we have 10,000 bombs. They are all over the world on land, sea and air. Every other country has less than a thousand all put together. So where is Osama (or some other zealot) most likely to get the bomb?

If 95% are in Russia or the U.S. we think you know the answer. But, wait a minute; powerful military forces secure those bombs. What chance is there that a crook would sell a bomb for $20,000,000? What chance is there that a spy or a traitor could steal a bomb? You might say Fat Chance but wait a minute.

Aren't the Russians the ones whose families are hungry and the soldiers who aren't getting paid? Well that is a problem in Russia, but you can count on our military and our scientists. We know they are just as efficient and honest as our Police or the corporations we work for Well, wait a minute. I hope they are better. Right!

The security people are only people so you can relate their morals and ability to the people you work with or our best military contractors like Halliburton. If they were guarding our 10,000 nuclear bombs what chance would there be that someone would goof up or take a 20 million dollar bribe?

Or to bring the issue right home, if your company was in charge of securing the bombs how secure would you feel?

Sorry, we didn't mean to keep you up tonight.

# THE $64 QUESTION
## AUGUST 12, 2005

We are at war to secure our supply of oil, but it seems the Chinese have more money and being a capitalistic nation we know what that means they get the oil. So the price zooms when the experts predicted it would go back to $40 a barrel. Now that we have broken through $64, $70 seems a better bet than $40. What does this mean?

1. *You pay more for everything and many buy less.*

2. *The oil companies earn more, and more and more.*

3. *We stay in Iraq.*

4. *Shiites establish Islamic law destroying a productive Arab society.*

5. *The Kurds get independence for a long-term lease on their oil fields.*

6. *The Sunnis end up with nothing in the new government plus no oil fields so they keep killing everyone.*

7. *George Bush says nothing.*

8. *Soldiers pray that George Bush knows what he is thinking.*

9. *The parents of the soldiers are afraid to think.*

10. *The typical American ignores the whole thing and worries about when the Cubs will win again.*

Other than that who cares about $64 oil we got bikes.

---

# THE POWER OF ONE OR THE LESSONS
# OF TIANANMEN SQUARE
# AUGUST 12, 2005

In the Chinese Political Uprising of 1989 one image probably stands out in your mind. It wasn't the thousands of protesting students but the photo of one man facing down a tank. Where the tank crew could crush a mob of a dozen protestors, they could not win the battle by crushing this one lone man he impacted public opinion around the world.

It is for this reason that the supporters of Cindy Sheehan made a big mistake.

Cindy was upset. She was sick of the war and wanted to ask the President why her son died. She was challenging the President and our entire government. And it was working.

One woman on a hot dusty road facing down the President of the United States. Nobody could move her without conceding her victory. The President was losing face and had no way to win. If he meets with her he loses. If he ignores her he loses. If she gets sick or hurt he loses. In the battle for public opinion she won.

Suddenly every opponent of the war and President Bush rushed to "support" her and share her idea. It has turned into a circus. Now her effective protest has become an event whose results will favor one side or the other, but the simplicity of her one woman protest is gone. The President got off the hook.

So we guess the moral is that you don't need a march of thousands to make your point. Pick your time carefully, pick your place carefully and let your voice be heard. It's called democracy.

Cindy did it right but she just had too many friends.

## THANK HEAVENS PAT APOLOGIZED
## AUGUST 24, 2005

Saying we should assassinate the President of Venezuela why he must think he is the President or something. Next thing you know Robertson will get out our old gunboats and do some good old-fashioned "diplomacy."

Seriously we have enough leaders talking about eliminating the Axis of Evil and other statements that make no possible sense. They just make us look bad. Everyone knows our history of Central and South America in overthrowing and assassinating leaders who don't go along with us.

We need the Venezuelan oil, but isn't there a better way than threatening to kill the President. Bush should remember Hugo Chavez is a close friend of Castro and what happened when Kennedy tried a dozen times to kill Castro some say Castro got tired of the game and returned the favor. It is not smart.

But it is too much when the religious supporters of the President think they should make these calls and get ahead of the President who just says Chavez is a danger.

And by the way didn't anyone tell Pat Congress passed a law to make that illegal so he should at least be discrete.

But in retrospect, Pat may be pretty smart. His TV audiences will probably double this week who knows what will be his next religious sermon.


## PRAY AND PAY
## AUGUST 30, 2005

Katrina has been more devastating than the reports and that is saying something. In fact it defies reporting. Only one word comes close hell.

Louisiana, Mississippi and Alabama do not have the money or ability to dig themselves out and rebuild. They need the financial support of the rest of the country, countless business organizations, insurance companies and of course big, big, big bucks from Uncle Sam.

Feeding and housing hundreds of thousands of people for months will be a challenge, but rebuilding the economy is a much bigger battle. Many businesses cannot recover and will just close. The tourist business will be hit for months or years. In general the economy will disintegrate.

The only salvation is reconstruction and the dollars it will generate. Insurance will only go so far the rest is going to have to come from the government.

Rebuilding Iraq will have a new and tougher competitor. Come to think of it they have a lot in common: excessive heat, no water, no electricity, looting, etc.

Unfortunately Congress just cut spending on flood controls and planning in Louisiana, and is in the process of cutting many domestic programs. Now they will have to reverse course and spend tens of billions to start getting the area even back on their feet. Those states voted for President Bush and his theory of individual responsibility but now it is the opposite. Congress is going to have to step up and assume the cost. So many poor people it is hard to imagine that they can ever make it on their own or repay the financing that will be necessary.

The pressure is on the President. He says FEMA is ready. But you can tell how it is going from watching the face of the Director of FEMA as the days progress. He looked confidant and relaxed yesterday. Check him out on Friday and then next month. Talk about a tough job.

Come to think of it, we better check out ourselves. It will be painful watching so many people suffer. And it only gets worse when you realize we are just going into the peak hurricane season.

## ONE GOOD THING ABOUT THE POWER BEING OUT IN NEW ORLEANS
## SEPTEMBER 1, 2005

This morning Diane Sawyer of ABC interviewed President Bush about New Orleans where thousands are fighting to survive. It is a good thing that the 100,000 people trapped in the city could not hear him. To put it kindly, it was pathetic and would have destroyed any hope they have for rescue and their future.

Karl Rove has to keep Bush away from interviews that expose his inability to understand and express himself. We have seen it many times, but this morning's interview should have been easy and it just ended up being sad.

There was no hope or plan discussed except moving 30,000 people into the Astrodome.

Instead, the President went back to individual responsibility which is tough when you had no money and no place to run to (like all the wealthy people) and now have no food or water and no sighting of any relief effort on the part of the city, state or federal government. They are trapped in a sinking city.

However, the President did say, "zero tolerance" for people breaking into stores for food or water and a bunch of other platitudes. But when Sawyer asked him about oil companies giving up a small percentage of their newfound profits, the President did not know what to say so he ignored the question.

All in all we are wondering if it would be better if our power was off for the next week. Can't take too many fireside chats like this one.

# TIME TO START PLANNING THE
# VICTIM COMPENSATION BILL
# SEPTEMBER 2, 2005

Obviously the President and Congress will want to compensate the families of the victims of Katrina. We paid millions to each family of the 9/11 disaster so it is the right thing to do when a terrible thing happens and innocent people lose their lives.

The Katrina victims probably will get much more than the 9/11 victims. After all in New York the attack was done by a few Saudis and the police and firemen died heroically trying to save the people. There was no delay and the Mayor let the rescue effort. In addition the survivor's homes and valuables were safe.

The Katrina victims are a result of a natural disaster but poor government planning and lack of response probably makes the federal government feel that they are more liable. After all not many died trying to save the trapped victims sure wasn't like 9/11).

A good suggestion probably is some flat fee like two or three million for a single person and four million for a married person and a million or so for each dependent child.

The good news is that probably Katrina's victims will be easier to settle with than the New Yorkers who demanded so much more.

Well you can count on President Bush being on top of this subject and we imagine the Senators will be rushing to get them name on the 2005 Katrina Victim Compensation Bill. Hope they can squeeze it in before the ban on estate tax bill.

You might ask are we kidding.

If you did we would answer of course.

But then we would ask you why?

## THE POLITICAL CAPITAL ACCOUNT IS EMPTY
## SEPTEMBER 4, 2005

When Bush and Cheney were reelected in November they said that they had earned a lot of political capital and that they were going to spend it. One key area was the Supreme Court and the appointment of conservative justices, which his supporters have demanded to outlaw abortion.

Unfortunately for him this capital has left his account in the form of a confusing and expensive war, oil shortages and now Katrina. Not much left to scare the opposition. His Presidency is wounded.

The death of Chief Justice Rehnquist could not have come at a worse time for the administration. The President has to get two Justices confirmed or if he tries to elevate Thomas or another justice to Chief then he will have three fights on his hands.

The country knows that the President's judgment is flawed and his influence in Washington and around the world is collapsing. The Democrats will have the power and confidence to oppose his agenda including the Supreme Court. They will go to the mat unless he nominates a moderate. The President will probably nominate a woman, black or Latino to help gain bipartisan support. It will be interesting and exciting to watch.

P.S. Where Is Dick?

We know that the President has limited abilities. But we also know he has top advisors including the Vice President. In the past Dick Cheney has guided the President and helped him through tough situations. Remember 9/11 when he effectively took charge as Bush was figuring out what was going on. Have you heard him say one word about Katrina or anything? If so we missed it.

Has he been helping in the relief effort? How about getting his friends at Halliburton who efficiently deployed thousands of people to Iraq on short notice. And instead of sending out the "Old Presidents" to raise private donations, Dick could do better in one hour on the phone.

Where is he? Is something wrong or has he given up on the President?

## UNFORTUNATELY, THE INCOMPETENCE IS IN ITS INFANCY
## SEPTEMBER 4, 2005

Katrina is a disaster that defies imagination and solutions are difficult for anyone to find. The next weeks will be filled with hundreds or thousands of bodies being found in homes and buildings. The public will be sick to their stomach and are going to expect Washington to get their act together. But unfortunately the Administration will probably continue their bumbling and fumbling.

First the administration is having a difficult time figuring out where to put the people who have nothing. Originally the buses didn't come because they had no place to take the people. How many football stadiums do they have in Texas? It will be a job for many cities.

Disease may be rampant and the government would like to send patients to hospitals all over the country. But few hospitals take in homeless patients on a long-term basis. And remember families come with the patient. Lots will offer short-term aid but few will assume the responsibility for ongoing care and support

The economy in Mississippi and Louisiana has been destroyed. No tax money coming in and no jobs for most of the people. We know how difficult it is to create jobs in normal times the burden on the states will be overwhelming.

Wealthy homes on the coast will be rebuilt but that is up to them and their insurance companies. The President is talking about rebuilding New Orleans and homes for hundreds of thousands of people who had no insurance and no assets. If it happens it will be long after George has gone back to Texas to build his library.

Possibly the toughest challenge is in schooling the children. The President has to step up and propose major legislation. Where they live with their parents and where they go to school will require courage and good thinking.

We could go on, but you get the idea. Promises are easy like "The troops are on the way." But if George Bush can't get his act together he will go down in history as our most uncaring and incompetent president.

The only person happy to see that would have been Herbert Hoover.


## A SAD CHAPTER, BUT NO SURPRISE
## SEPTEMBER 8, 2005

Several Updaters have questioned the meaning of our comment that "the buses didn't come to the Super Dome because they had no place to go."

It really is simple. If you were a tourist the government brought in buses in and took you to a hotel or airport in Texas. No one stopped them. There were many other buses but they didn't know where they would be allowed to deliver their poor survivors.

In effect many cities did not want the survivors in their town or were afraid of them. Those survivors who tried to walk out of New Orleans were fired upon and made to go back by the police forces of the other cities. You won't find this simple fact in major media reports but the stories are all over the world and the Internet. Attached is a link to one first-hand view.
http://www.truthout.org/docs_2005/090805A.shtml

The situation has not changed. Thousands are still waiting at the Astrodome for a place that will accept them. In the meantime, private security forces are being brought in to help protect the cities from Katrina's poor, black and sick survivors. Residents are buying guns to protect themselves.

These comments should not negate the fantastic efforts of thousands of wonderful people, churches and cities that have opened their hearts. Just remember others don't have a brain or a heart. Racism is not a political matter; it is a fact of life.

The buses didn't come because they had no place to go. No one would take them. It is a massive problem that we all need to work to resolve.

If this reminds you of a ship with survivors looking for a place to dock before the start of WWII, you were not surprised.

## LETTER FROM CORA HOOPER
## SEPTEMBER 11, 2005

Dear Mr. Update:

Up to the hurricane your Updates were interesting and somewhat fair. Since Katrina you seem to put all the blame on President Bush. This is wrong. He is a good man from a good family. Jeb is smarter and hopefully he will be our next president, but George cares for people and is fighting to protect us from terrorists.

I am sure the President is also doing his best to help the poor people of Mississippi and Louisiana. But there are difficult issues:

1. *Where do you house poor people with no money? Most of the people in our town have contributed generously to the Red Cross. But you cannot expect us to accept the Katrina refugees in our town. Those people had serious problems before this tragedy, as I am sure you know if you visited New Orleans in recent years. It may not be their fault but our town won't feel safe if they are here. That is why so many of our law-abiding citizens are buying guns to protect their homes and families.*

2. *You mentioned disease. Normally when a large group of people is exposed to serious diseases, they are quarantined. If we bring them into town we will be exposed. They should be sent to government hospitals somewhere. And if they are in hospital can we expect Washington to pay for their care.*

3. *The children certainly need to be helped, but should we put them in our schools. Their background and educational level is so different that it would disrupt our schools. We do have a special needs facility in our town and that might be a place where we could set up a school if it was necessary. But it is not ideal to say the least.*

4. *Finding jobs for the adults would be all but impossible. We have a lot of unemployed people already from our factory that closed and no shortage of people wanting menial work. In fact we have quite a few Hispanic immigrants that work very hard for minimum wage jobs. How could we handle this influx on unskilled people?*

5. *Finally there is cost. Congress is appropriating billions, but you can never count on it getting down to our level. We could be stuck with supporting and caring for these people for years.*

No, this is not the President's fault, but Congress should figure out how to help the poor people by building new housing in appropriate secluded areas. We will pay our share with taxes to help them get on their feet so they can become productive members of society.

I do hope they understand that Individual responsibility it still the way of life in our society. Once they are back on their feet they will have to take care of themselves, just like we do. I know you criticize the President for this philosophy but it makes perfect sense to me.

I could go on, but I hope you can see that this is a case of serious social questions. I used to be an acting mayor and know how our people feel. They are charitable and believe in helping thy neighbor but cannot be asked to change their way of life because of a natural catastrophe.

One more point. I resented the attack on President Hoover. In the Hurricane of 1927 he did a wonderful job and the depression was not his fault.

Respectfully yours,

Cora H. Hooper

# PRESSURE ON THE PRESIDENCY
## SEPTEMBER 17, 2005

It was a historic speech and the President's power and place in history was in the balance. Unfortunately he seemed to be swinging wildly.

Certainly Bush had to balance his image of not caring for the victims. He needed to demonstrate his resolve and compassion, but his speech raised the bar very high and promised everything conceivable. Now his problems have multiplied.

First there are three groups in Washington the liberals, the fiscal conservatives and the ones who are joyfully rubbing their hands at the opportunity to make money. Right now the liberals and the conservatives do not believe that the President can do what he promised. He could face a tough sell in Congress.

Second, he took" personal responsibility for the solution." The President should have appointed a nationally known administrator or at least a more intelligent "Brownie" to take the fall later.

No matter how well a job he does the victims and the public will probably not be pleased with the programs or progress. There is so much to do and his administration is not efficient in managing public programs.

Finally, the President will leave the country with a historic debt that will hang around his party's neck for years. He is afraid to raise taxes or end the war so the billions will be taken from other programs. Less health, education and welfare will be the rule.

On our first Katrina Update we predicted how the mess would wear on Mr. Brown. Now we should start watching how the mess shows up on the face of our President.

It is amazing how nature and a few mistakes can change history and we still have three years to go.

---

## FEMA MOVES INTO HIGH GEAR
## WITH POLITICAL CONTRACTS
## SEPTEMBER 24, 2005

If there is anything other than a war that gets the Washington corruption machine moving it is Hurricanes. Katrina and Rita present the opportunity and FEMA is up to the job.

No one would have picked Mike Brown to be President of a major corporation, say like Halliburton, but he was the ideal person to head FEMA. He didn't know anything about emergency planning but he sure knew who should get the contracts. Now that he is gone it is a little more difficult but they still have all the money people and the former FEMA director, Joe Allbaugh to show the way. Joe is now a lobbyist who has the amazing ability to get contracts for his clients. I guess his skill is in identifying the very best and honest companies to do the work or something like that.

Last week Newsweek documented listed these contracts. There of course was Halliburton who does not have to share their profit with Joe as they have a direct connection but Joe got Shaw 200 million, Bechtel 103 million (just to get going) and it goes on and on. Turn over a rock and you see why the firms got the contract. You sure can see why some of the people in DC love Katrina.

Anyway no one seems to care except some of the local contractors who are sitting idly by while outside firms go to work on their city. The average citizen is too busy, too stupid or too jaded to care.

This story of corruption in Washington is not news. However it is humorous when these same politicians get very emotional about corruption in the UN and corrupt dictators stealing from their people. We sure don't see any concern about the hundred million dollar contracts flying out to their "friends or would the word "partners" be more correct.

In any event, wasn't that what "Brownie" was really good at.

---

# FOUR LADIES WHO CAN CHANGE HISTORY
# SEPTEMBER 25, 2005

In 1997 the Senate voted 95-0 to not join the Kyoto Treaty on Greenhouse Gases. Since then the world has made great progress to control the environment with only the US and one other country in denial. In recent years many Senators have changed their minds and major corporations are moving forward on a voluntary basis but the President remains firmly against this environmental law.

Katrina has made believers out of a lot of people from Florida to Texas; I guess five feet of water in your house gives you cause to study the subject. In any event you can expect the President to start "reviewing the situation." His party will help him see the wisdom of laws to conserve energy.

The second is Barbara Bush who has taken a lot of flak for her comments about the poor people of New Orleans having nothing to begin with so how bad can Katrina be for them. Some commentators have used this to accuse the President's entire family of racism. Well no one knows what is in her heart, but at least Barbara is aware that many black people have absolutely nothing. This is better than many upstanding citizens and leaders that keep their eyes wired shut so they do not see this obvious fact. Give Barbara a break; she may be educating the country.

And this weekend Cindy and Rita competed for the same head-line. One was less than expected (thankfully) and one was more than expected. Rita did a lot of damage but much less than we feared. Washington could breathe a sigh of relief and hope that the Hurricane season will end soon. However Cindy Shehan who started out as a one-woman protest to see the President led a 100,000-person march in Washington. In a month filled with na-tional disasters, this massive March is causing the administration a big headache. They can only imagine how many protestors the next march will draw as Iraq still seems to be a no win situation.

---

# IT'S SATURDAY MORNING AND TIME TO PLAY LETS PRETEND! OCTOBER 1, 2005

If you are over 60 you probably had some very important education every Saturday morning listening to the radio show called Let's Pretend. If so you are prepared to read our newspapers and enjoy Let's Pretend news.. You know the stories that are total nonsense. For example play Let's Pretend with today's paper:

1. *Let's pretend that retiring General Myers deserves all the praise he received for leading our Army leading our war in Iraq as National Guard Pfc. England deserves her three-year prison term for abusing prisoners.*

2. *Let's Pretend that reporter Judith Miller was protecting the rights of Journalists as she spent three months in prison and that it took her all that time to understand that Scooter Libby had released her from her promise of confidentiality. Playing Let's Pretend is better than thinking that it took them three months to get their story straight before testifying to the Grand Jury.*

3. *And while talking about the Valerie (Wilson) Plumb case, Let's Pretend the President really meant what he said when he vowed to fire anyone involved in this leak that probably cost the lives of many agents. Well you can't blame him as who would have guessed that his key advisors would get caught.*

4. *Let's Pretend that all the people supporting Tom Delay believe he is innocent. After all he seems to be accused of many crimes so it probably one of those "political things."*

5. *Let's Pretend that Bill Bennett's comments about the best way to reduce crime was to abort all Black babies was just an "unfortunate illustration" and has nothing to do with Katrina or the race issue that is now front and center in the country. And while we are on the subject Let's Pretend that the next thing Bill's supporters do not say is how many Blacks are in prison.*

6. *Let's Pretend that Senator Frisk didn't know that his family's business was going bad when he sold all his HCA stock and saved millions of dollars. Why he couldn't be as guilty as that ex con Martha Stewart could he?*

7. *Let's Pretend that the billions we spent on FEMA since 9/11'was properly and effectively used. Congress could have another exciting hearing with Brownie to ascertain how he managed the money.*

8. *Let's Pretend that the House did not know how viciously they were cutting funding for hundreds of thousands of poor people when they left for vacation yesterday. And Let's Pretend that they will rush back to Washington to correct the error like they did to protect one sick person, Terri Schiavo.*

Oh well. Our half hour of fun and fantasy is over. Children remember to listen to your Mother and Father and always tell the truth. See you next Saturday.


## TALK ABOUT DUMMYING DOWN THE SUPREME COURT
## OCTOBER 5, 2005

Don't see how the confirmation of Harriet Miers can be stopped but it is certainly making for interesting politics. Both sides prefer an intelligent and experienced person on the court no matter what their views as people can learn and change. It is another thing to have a justice who has little ability or experience.

The only reason the President nominated her is that his administration is in trouble that is growing by the day and may take many more major hits (Iraq, Valerie Wilson, DeLay, Blunt, Prisoner Abuse, Deficit, etc.) during the confirmation process. He needs a person who the Democrats will not attack and is telling his supporters that his administration's problems come first. It is amazing how political events can change the history of our country for decades.

But the Republicans will not go quietly. They will ask more questions about abortion than the Democrats. The Democrats will ask if she has told the president her views on abortion. But the Republicans may want to know if she knows the President's opinion on abortion. They are beginning to get the feeling that they have been hustled on this subject and the President is doing the same thing he did with same sex marriage just a ploy for the people to vote for him, but no intention of doing anything about it.

It is especially fun to listen to Talk Radio. Progressive radio doesn't know what to say. Should they attack or just watch the battle between the President and his party. The Conservative programs like Rush, have to listen to their supporters tell them to quit complaining and support the President. What fun.

And then some interesting comments like Ms. Miers that George Bush is the smartest person she ever met. We will let you evaluate that comment.

In any event the Republicans cannot vote against her without telling the world that they do not think George is honest or competent. And the Democrats will figure that this incompetent judge might do less damage to their agenda than the next person he would nominate. It is not the ideal way to be confirmed but

Welcome aboard, Supreme Court Justice Miers.

# KAMIKAZE WHITE HOUSE
# OCTOBER 11, 2005

If your brain didn't tell you otherwise, you would have to believe that some power is determined to destroy the Presidency or the White House is on a Kamikaze mission.

- *Could it be that the VP has lost control?*

- *Could it be a Democrat Double Agent?*

- *Could it be a Republican who wants to even the score with the Bush family?*

- *Could it be the Chinese or maybe the Saudi's?*

- *Could it be that the President no longer trusts his advisors?*

- *Could it be that the pressure has clouded the President's mind?*

There must be reason.

No one could send the President out with such weak speeches or terrible answers to questions that are obvious. The supportive press throws him a softball question and he misses it. The Senate and the House is out of control with corruption and extensive spending. The choice for Supreme Court was sad guaranteed to be liked by no one and hated by many. The war policy is too messy to even comment on. The delayed action and then extensive promises on Katrina are amazing.

We hate to say this but the most obvious answer is that the mastermind of the Presidency, Karl Rove is focused on saving himself from the Special Prosecutor and doesn't have time to help Bush handle each situation.

With Rove too busy, the President has decided to make his own decisions and what we are seeing for the first time is the real Presidency of George Bush.

Many people in Washington do not believe that George will let Karl resign even if he is indicted next week. Although we all know the dirty tricks Rove has played on opponents and the country, we better hope this is the case. What an amazing situation.

The country needs Karl Rove in the Oval Office.

## ALL ROVES LEAD TO THE WHITE HOUSE: PART 2 OCTOBER 22, 2005

Laying Low The Vice President Is Using an Old Chicago Technique!

When the Chicago Police were after a gangster the usual technique was to leave town and lay low hoping that the cops would find someone else to bother.

VP Cheney has been laying low for a long time. Other than fund raisers and when the President ordered him to the Gulf for damage control or officially to "take charge" of Katrina relief did you see him. The Katrina tour of duty ended in a couple days when a hurricane victim told him on camera to go perform "an impossible physical act."

As we reported in the July 6th Update, "All Roves Lead to the White House" that Karl and Scooter didn't orchestra the program to discredit Wilson without approval from the President and or the Vice President. It was a White House plan to protect the phony CIA reports they used to attack Iraq. They felt they had to discredit Wilson or see their story and their war go up in smoke. The VP was probably calling the signals and who knows if the President was involved or just ignored.

In Illinois Fitzgerald convicted one person after another and for a lighter sentence they testified for the prosecution. Now our former Republican Governor is on trial with his most trusted aides testifying against him. The same pattern is being followed in Chicago and this week another person in the City Democratic corruption scandals was sentenced to only one year in prison. Many aides will tell the truth to avoid heavy prison time. The truth on the Valerie Wilson attack will come out. Not everyone is ready to fall on his or her sword to save Cheney.

But now the pressure is on Fitzgerald. Karl and Scooter are history whether or not they are indicted. But do you indict a Vice President of the United States? Impeaching Clinton hurt the country and possibly set the stage for 9/11 and all that followed. An indictment of Cheney is much more serious and the damage to our country will be much more serious. The result will be a "dead duck" President for three more years in a very dangerous world.

The ball is in Fitzgerald's court and the game is about to begin.


## ALL ROVES LEAD TO
## THE WHITE HOUSE: PART 3
## OCTOBER 22, 2005

The New York Times Bites the Dust

The casualties in the Valerie Wilson case continue to grow and this time it is the mighty New York Times. For generations this journalism giant has been the beacon of knowledge and truth. Now the paper will go down in history for fabricating reasons to start the Iraq war.

Judith Miller is not the problem. Her reporting and story about going to jail for journalistic freedom will be laughed at and forgotten. She will find a new career with Halliburton or some other friendly corporation, as they certainly don't want her writing the truth in a future "tell all" book that is sure to come.

But the Times will pay a high price and questions will be raised for years as to how veteran editors could be taken in by so obviously planted stories or worse whether top management was in on the con with the Bush Administration.

Who could have imagined this would all come from a harebrained idea in the Vice President's office over a criticism from Ambassador Wilson that could have been ignored. And there is so much more to come.

## ALL ROVES LEAD TO
## THE WHITE HOUSE: PART 4
## OCTOBER 24, 2005

Open Season in Washington

At the start of each hunting season hunters decide whether to kill their prey with a Bow and Arrow, Rifle or Shotgun. However it seems that the Bush hunting season has opened in Washington and the weapon of choice is the Howitzer Cannon.

The biggest names in the Republican Hierarchy are attacking with charges that the country is being run by idiots, traitors and fascists. Read the articles and listen to the interviews and you will be amazed. Powerful Republicans like General Brent Scowcroft, close friend and National Security Advisor to Bush (the first) and former (?) close friend to VP Cheney and Secretary of State Rice are painting a picture that is far worse than any Bush basher has had the courage to say. And this is before Fitzgerald offers a report or indicts anyone.

The administration's few defenders have nothing to say except to start personal attacks on the Special Prosecutor and give Saturday Night Live more material for their satire.

The ship has sunk and everyone is fighting to get into the lifeboats.

But whatever your politics there is a danger. Many American who by and large do not listen or think about politics other than possibly voting every four years will hear these charges and could lose faith in their government. We found that great when it was in the Soviet Union; but scary if it could happen to us. Who is going to run the government? Who is going to lead Congress? Who is going to keep our country secure? Who is going to win or end the war? And most of all can Bush maintain his mental balance under this type of attack?

Anything that Special Prosecutor Fitzgerald does will be comparatively small compared to the damage of these howitzers fired by former supporters and friends. The Howitzers not only make a lot of noise but they inflict a lot of damage. Walter Reed better open up a new wing. There will be a lot of casualties in the next few days.

## IS THAT YOU COLIN?
## OCTOBER 26, 2005

Last week a speech by Col. Wilkerson, Secretary of State Colin Powell's former Chief of Staff included serious charges against the Bush administration, but then gave us a warning. We believe that Col Wilkerson may have been expressing the views of his old boss and thus it is worth listening carefully to his comments.

Here are some excerpts from the article and pay particular attention to the last paragraph remembering Powell's warning to Bush about the Pottery House Rule: If you break it you own it.

"We have courted disaster in Iraq, in North Korea, in Iran," said Mr. Wilkerson. "Generally, with regard to domestic crises like Katrina, Rita we haven't done very well on anything like that in a long time. And if something comes along that is truly serious, something like a nuclear weapon going off in a major American city, or something like a major pandemic, you are going to see the ineptitude of this government in a way that will take you back to the Declaration of Independence."

"The case that I saw for four-plus years was a case that I have never seen in my studies of aberrations, bastardizations, perturbations, changes to the national security decision-making process. What I saw was a cabal between the vice president of the United States, Richard Cheney, and the secretary of defense, Donald Rumsfeld, on critical issues that made decisions that the bureaucracy did not know were being made."

"When the time came to implement the decisions, said Mr. Wilkerson, "they were presented in such a disjointed, incredible way that the bureaucracy often didn't know what it was doing as it moved to carry them out."

Where was the president? According to Mr. Wilkerson, "You've got this collegiality there between the secretary of defense and the vice president, and you've got a president who is not versed in international relations and not too much interested in them either."

But here is the critical part he tells us we must stay the course.

"While not "evaluating the decision to go to war," Mr. Wilkerson told his audience that under the present circumstances "we can't leave Iraq. We simply can't." In his view, if American forces were to pull out too quickly, the U.S. would end up returning to the Middle East with "five million men and women under arms" within a decade.

Our guess is that is Colin is now running the Pottery Barn and has just told the American people that unfortunately you broke Iraq and it is yours!

10/26/05 after the sweep

# ALL ROVES LEAD TO
# THE WHITE HOUSE: PART 5
# OCTOBER 29, 2005

One Tough Hombre!

Libby's indictment is not being analyzed correctly in the media. Of course the White House Spin Machine is turning black to white and don't miss the opportunity to listen to the nonsense that no crime was committed it is fun. But once again the media does not seem to be doing their homework.

Scooter was selected to fall on his sword. He will have to run the risk of major jail time if he does not plea-bargain and put the mess in the Vice Presidents lap.

Fitzgerald is following his usual pattern. First he convicts the obvious crimes like Libby's perjury and during the trial Rove, the VP and more officials will have to testify probably again lying to protect themselves. The testimony will open up new charges. Remember in Illinois Fitzgerald convicted dozens of people (starting with truck drivers) before he was ready to take on the real target, Gov. George Ryan, a popular politician and Nobel Price nominee who is now on trial. We are at the beginning of the Wilson inquiry.

Scooter helped run the country and this is a big loss. He is tough to replace.

Most important the indictment now puts the President's reasons for war at major risk. Difficult for Bush to be fighting a war while the courts are saying you manufactured the whole thing.

A court finding of guilt or evidence disclosed in the trial could open the door to civil suits against the President and Vice President. It was the Right Wing's civil suits that drove Clinton crazy after the Impeachment was over. The Left Wing will want to return the favor as soon as possible and we don't think Bush and Cheney will do as good a job as Clinton in surviving such pressure.

---

The rank and file of the CIA who demanded this investigation in the beginning is working behind the scene to get even with many of the politicians who sold them down the river. Just as with "Deep Throat" and Nixon, the CIA no doubt has more bombshells to drop. And don't listen to the reports that Valerie was not a spy we will never know. The CIA could not tell the truth whether she was or wasn't without harming many agents.

The President is stonewalling the whole thing. It won't work. He and Cheney are going to have to face the public and admit their mistakes in not finding out the truth. More cover-ups will only make the situation more explosive.

 Well, the story will be with us for years. The President will try to create firestorms to get rid of it, but it won't work. A stain on a dress brought Clinton to the brink of destruction and now a little "routine" dirty work is bringing down their successor. And one final piece of advice to the White House: don't get Fitzgerald mad. He is one tough Hombre!

## THE PRESIDENT IS IN A TAG TEAM MATCH WITHOUT A PARTNER
## OCTOBER 30, 2005

President Bush is rushing out the next Supreme Court Nominee to get the Scooter Indictment off the front page, but he has a problem. The newly empowered Conservative wing of the Republicans and the newly encouraged Liberal wing of the Democrats have formed a tag team that is tough to beat. Both think they are the toughest act in town.

If he doesn't go to a proven anti-abortion nominee he will get in big trouble with the people who destroyed Harriet Miers. But if he does the Conservatives tag the Liberals and then they start the beating.

Bush is a damaged President and somehow has to get a candidate that is acceptable to both sides or expect an explosive situation. The Democrats are feeling their oats and could join forces with McCain's Gang (you could call them the referee) and defeat the Nuclear Option of changing the voting rules. Even if Bush wins the Nuclear Option, this would doom any Democratic cooperation on his future agenda and we have seen how so many important programs like social security have met the dust.

There must be days when George feels like throwing in the towel.

## BUSH ORDERS ETHICS AND SECURITY COURSE A LITTLE LATE AND PROBABLY NOT NECESSARY NOVEMBER 5, 2005

This morning the papers report that the President ordered security education for the White House staff. This probably is a good idea but the military has always had a short cut to teach the same subject. The first time someone discloses classified information to anyone that does not have a need to know that information –whether or not they have security clearance– they have a court martial and the person probably ends up in Leavenworth. The learning curve comes very fast.

So while Ethics and Security Education for the White House is probably a good idea, if Scooter goes to prison for five years they won't need this classroom experience.

## DEMOCRATS LOOKING FOR THE
## IRAQ EXIT DOOR
## NOVEMBER 5, 2005

The current turmoil in Washington may set the stage for key Democrats to "rescind" their vote giving the President power to go to war. They hope that the troubles of Rove, Libby, Cheney and the phony intelligence will give them a chance to formally bail out of the War and you might say leave it to George.

These Democrats are now getting warmed up to run for President or reelection and need to rewrite history. They want to pretend that they were misled or lied to. Probably some of this is true, but when you are an experienced politician like Colin Powell in the Administration or John Kerry in the opposition it is tough to believe they were misled.

Many knew George and his neocons were going to attack Iraq and that 9/11 was just a convenient excuse. Only a handful of Congress had the courage to oppose the President, The rest went along hoping for the best. Now that the worse has happened, they are looking for the exit door and hope the public continues to not pay attention and live in ignorance.

## ALL ROVES LEAD TO
## THE WHITE HOUSE: PART 6
## NOVEMBER 12, 2005

Scooter Has a Tough Decision

The Prosecutor is asking him to give up Rove and/or Cheney in order to get a reduced sentence in a plea bargain. If Libby turns it down he takes a chance that other people not yet indicted will give the info to save their own skin. In addition, the Senate Intelligence Committee may have more info that makes Scooter's info unimportant. Then he will go to trial.

Of course he can hope that the jury will find him not guilty but with his own notes as evidence and this tough prosecutor plus a Washington area jury, he can't count on it.

Let's say he gets five years. Then all that is left is to sit in prison waiting for George to pardon him the way Ford pardoned Nixon. He might be waiting a long time If George's Presidency is in the trouble it is in now; pardoning Scooter could be the icing on the cake of his failed presidency.

Scooter has a lot to think about. His testimony and get out of jail card are perishable.

'Your Credit Card is Overdrawn'

Let's say there is a message on your phone and it is the Chinese American Express Company. "Your daughter's credit card is overdrawn by $27,166.96 and the interest is growing every hour. Please arrange payment immediately to avoid late charges."

Sort of scary. How are you going to get her out of the mess?

Uh Oh another call from the same guy. "You, your spouse and all your kids also have the same problem each owes $27,166.96 and we want payment."

The simple fact is that according to the National Debt Clock the national debt tonight is $27,166.96 for every American man, woman and child.

If this doesn't scare you, you probably go around humming "Whatever will be will be."

Our Congress and President have to take a deep breath and admit that they don't know what they are doing and start all over. China and other countries control our debt and our destiny.

Our children and their children deserve a better fate.

## ARE THERE SOME THINGS WE CAN ALL AGREE ON? NOVEMBER 14, 2005

- *Keeping people locked up without any outside contact is wrong*

- *Never charging prisoners with a crime is wrong.*

- *Using wild charges that the prisoner is an enemy of civilized people is wrong.*

- *Mocking the religion of Muslim prisoners is wrong.*

- *Torture of prisoners is wrong.*

- *Secret courts and arbitrary sentences are wrong.*

- *Prisoners dying in prison without ever coming to trial is wrong.*

Well we could go on and on but you get the idea. All this and much more was done legally in the Spanish Inquisition over 500 years ago. It created animosity between countries and religions that lives to this day.

Unfortunately it seems to be difficult to learn from history. Last week the Senate voted 49 to 42 for the Graham Amendment giving the President unfettered power to hold prisoners at Guantanamo Bay for the rest of their lives, with no criminal charges and no right to challenge their confinement by Habeas Corpus.

Wonder how history will judge us.

## ALL ROVES LEAD TO
## THE WHITE HOUSE: PART 7
## NOVEMBER 17, 2005

The Post Joins the Times in the Toilet

The story is amazing. Bob Woodward, of the Washington Post, hides critical information on the Valerie Plame case from everyone for two years or invents a story to protect his sources.

In a short time we will find out more, but are beginning to think that this is like going to the Movie Adventure Serials when we were kids. Every Saturday's segment ended with a cliffhanger that no one could imagine how our hero would escape.Back then the price of admission was 25 cents. These days the country is paying is a little more in loss of confidence and respect for political leaders and the press.

We are beginning to feel sorry for the President.nothing good is going his way and indirectly for the country. But tonight our concern is for independent journalism as two of our leading newspapers have been exposed to either be giving us phony news or covering up serious crimes.

We expect this type of nonsense from political hacks on the radio and third-rate papers, but if the only way leading reporters can get a story is by selling their soul to "confidential sources" they should take a night course in Reporting 101.

Well kids this is really exciting, don't miss next week's serial titled "The Terrible Prosecutor Attacks Public Radio."

# The End of 2005

## MARSHALL DILLON, LONE RANGER AND HOPALONG CASSIDY MOVE OVER PATRICK IS THE NEW LAW MAN IN TOWN... NOVEMBER 18, 2005

It won't be long before there will be a TV Series about the toughest gun fighter in the country none other than the Special Prosecutor Patrick Fitzgerald. He takes on the toughest and most powerful people in our society without concern or care. Presidents, Governors, Mayors, Member of the House of Lords, Mafia Leader, etc., make no difference to Patrick. The only question is did you break the law? This is a tough standard for most of our Politicians and Corporate Executives who are used to getting away with a lot of shady deals.

All of us know about the White House and the damage caused by Patrick's indictment of Scooter, an investigation that goes right to the heart of the national debate on whether the administration lied to the country about going to war. In Illinois our former and internationally respected Republican Governor is weeks away from being convicted and going to prison. Richard Daley, the most powerful Mayor in the country is circling the wagons as one after another city official is rolling over to get a small one or two year sentence in exchange for testifying against their bosses.

Today Patrick indicted Conrad Black a British citizen and member of the House of Lords for massive fraud in the Hollinger News-paper Empire a case that affects the news we get in many major cities. As usual Black's VP will be testifying against him to hold his sentence down to six years.

When Fitzgerald gets you in his sights there is only one thing to do make sure you have good supply of Depends. You will need them.

## TALK ABOUT TROUBLE IN THE FAMILY.
## BREAKING RANKS
## NOVEMBER 19, 2005

In the October 27th Update we wondered if former Secretary of State Colin Powell was getting his views across by using his Chief of Staff Col. Wilkerson as a surrogate.

Now it seems that Bush 41 is doing the same with Brent Scow-croft, his Former National Security Advisor. In a long interview in the October 31st edition of The New Yorker Magazine Scowcroft publicly attacked the President's policy on Iraq.

Our thanks to our good friend Hal for sending us the article titled "Breaking Ranks."

If this is the fact (and we emphasize if) then things are worse than most of us want to believe. Bush 41 does not approve of the way Bush 43 is running the company store. And he does not want his reputation to go down the drain with his son.

I guess every family has some problem.

And if your father talking against you is not bad enough it seems that the President's military support is crumbling. Rep. Murtha's call for redeployment in Iraq is a major challenge. Since he is a friend of the military it must mean a change in the Pentagon's view of the war. They never respected the Secretary of Defense but now must think that his policy and plan must change.

It reminds us of Katrina. The storm was a category three until warm water in the Gulf turned it into the terrible category five killer. The Stop the War crowd was growing slowly without direction but Thursday when Rep. Murtha joined the attack the movement became a category 5 headache for the President.

As we saw last night in House of Representatives, Murtha cannot be silenced or effectively attacked. His view will now get more attention than ever in the press and in Congress.

## DELVING INTO THE GI MIND
## NOVEMBER 29, 2005

It is rather pathetic to hear so many politicians talking about the morale of our Soldiers and Marines in Iraq. First it is not like an election where you are going to be able to accurately judge the feelings of so many individuals. The morale of a professional officer would be quite different than a National Guard mother with two small children back home. But as long as we hear these comments, the Update would like to add a few thoughts:

- *Morale is the responsibility of each Unit's Commanding Officer. If he or she does a good job their morale will be good. If not then they will neither do a good job nor have a positive outlook on their service.*

- *Soldiers are not paid to think or judge their mission so they probably don't spend much time on the news, politics, etc. They concentrate on doing their job that day. If you were in 120-degree heat with someone trying to kill you, morale would not be your big concern.*

- *Obviously every GI wants to believe in their mission. If not every day would be torture. There is plenty of time when they return home to think about whether it was a noble mission or just a bad dream. No one wants to serve or die in vain.*

- *For the Commanders it was obvious from the beginning of this war that Rumsfield was in charge and disagreeing with him was the fast way to end your career. So don't listen to the Generals about the morale of their troops. If a General said it was poor he or she would be relieved of their command.*

- *The only key we now have on morale is the reenlistment rate. The bonuses for reenlistment have climbed sky high but still if you do not believe in the mission, you will get out as fast as they let you. Since many are reenlisting morale is probably as good as you could expect.*

- *Finally, we will all know the truth about morale in three or four years as the Veterans return to civilian life. Their thoughts on the war will be obvious just as it was in WWII (very high), Korea (50 50) and Viet Nam (very low). So far there have only been a few fragging and desertion cases reported so it hasn't reached the level of Viet Nam.*

In the meantime, let's hope and pray that they will come home safe with their biggest problem having been poor morale.


## POLITICIANS CAN TALK BUT PRESIDENTS MUST ACT
## DECEMBER 4, 2005

You can divide politicians into two categories. Those that think they could be President and those that know they can't. It is much easier to tell us what should be done if they never are going to have to follow their own advice.

If you think you might be President then someday you might have to follow your own advice and that could be a big problem. Think about Franklin Roosevelt saying that he would not get involved in the War in Europe in his 1936 campaign. Trying to get out of that campaign promise almost changed history and could have allowed Hitler to conquer all of Europe before we were lucky enough for Japan to attack.

Iraq is a classic case in point. Maybe we should not have invaded Iraq but now that the damage has been done we will stay to protect our oil supply from the Middle East. It is easy for a senator that has only his or her own constituents to worry about to talk about "withdrawing all troops" or "stay the course." No one will pay attention to what they say.

However if you are Senator McCain or Senator Clinton you might have to make that decision in three years. You can say the same about every issue. The President must not only talk but do and history will judge them. Better watch what you say as it can come back to haunt you.

That being said, we do believe that the full national discussion on the war is good for democracy and the country. The President's first report on Iraq was pathetic. We can only assume that Karl is working full time on staying out of prison and is letting the President write his own talks.

Bush has three more speeches on Iraq and he must present a more intelligent and honest case for the war. You might want to listen closely for the hint that we will be there for as long as oil is under the sand. The real war in the future will be for that oil and the enemy will be much, much tougher. It is a five-letter word starting with "C."

Don't expect this much honesty from George but you can look for a few clues.

## ARE THESE JUST A FEW BAD APPLES?
## DECEMBER 10, 2005

There are so many corruption cases that it is easy to get overwhelmed and close our eyes to the whole subject. But many affect our nation.

Congressman Cunningham from San Diego is a good case because it covers everything bad you can imagine. It involves officials in the military, Congressional Defense and Intelligence committees, etc. To refresh your memory he forced the Pentagon to buy a product that they did not want from the MZM Corporation. This certainly makes a joke out of Congress supporting our troops, or maybe that is just in third place after supporting their bribers.

Most crooks try to cover up their tracks. They are careful to hide the payoff get a third party to get the money. Not in this deal. They made straight money payoffs on the public record. Cheap things like paying for his daughter's graduation party and buying a Rolls Royce plus the one that did them in the company bought Cunningham's house for $1,700,000. And then in a few months sold it for something like $800,000 (the real value). And who caught this payoff that was public knowledge. The Inspector General of the Army? The Special Prosecutor? The Congressional Ethics committee? NO.

It was a small town newspaper reporter going over the real estate sales. If we truly wanted to stop corruption our country should honor this reporter.

There was no concern on the Congressman or MZM's part that they would be caught. This should give us all cause to think. Was it because everyone in a position of power in Washington knew what they were doing and could care less?

Cunningham has pleaded guilty to taking $2,400,000 in bribes from MZM Corporation, but the justice system is probably going to let him off easy with a sentence of two or three years. (Much less than many DUI accident drivers get). The President of MZM has not gone to trial. So far no one has checked out any other deals that Cunningham was working on or should we believe this was his one discretion. And has anyone checked out other officials that promoted MZM's case?

Well you can go on and on looking for corruption in Washington. But if you think about this case for a few minutes it becomes obvious. This is not a case of a few bad apples

It is a rotten Apple Orchard!

## IS CHENEY ON TRIAL?
## DECEMBER 11, 2005

It seems that there is an unofficial trial going on in Washington. The defendant is VP Cheney, the prosecutor is Senator McCain and the Judge is George Bush. The charge is war crimes. And the trial is being conducted in the Senate under the guise of the McCain amendment (prohibiting torture) to the military appropriations bill.

Some may say that this is a theoretical battle over future policy regarding the role of torture in our society, but it is more imminent. International organizations may charge our country with War Crimes with the chief architect being VP Cheney.

Many Republicans are abandoning the President and Cheney on this issue either having the same moral principal that McCain has or feel that this issue will bring them down with Cheney. At this point they are checking his medical bulletins in hopes of an excuse for him to resign. In the meantime Bush has four choices:

Bush says he will veto the military appropriations bill if it includes the McCain amendment, but that is risky business. The Senate is lined up with McCain.

Bush can go along with the amendment and change our policy on torture and secret prisons. That would get the bill passed but would not solve the problems of the past violations.

Bush can issue a ruling that would exonerate all previous torturers and say the new law applies from now on. But Bush remembers what happened to President Ford when he pardoned Nixon. Neither the country or the world took him seriously after that event, although it obviously was the right thing for the country

And finally Bush can just continue the political tightrope like sending Condie out to double talk Europe but that was a disaster and would not placate the Senate.

Well once again it is exciting and at least the Historians will be able to write a dozen books on the subject.

## IF YOU KICK A DOG DON'T BE SURPRISED WHEN YOU GET BIT
## DECEMBER 19, 2005

Last week the President rightfully focused on the successful election in Iraq and planned on taking a big step forward in regaining the momentum of his administrative program. But a funny thing happened on the way to the victory party the traditional media (networks, real newspapers, etc.) counter attacked.

First with the backing of many journalists conservative Republicans joined Democrats to block the Patriot Act. Now the President will have to fight to get this critical part of his program back on track.

Then John McCain with tremendous help from the media brought the White House to their knees over the torture amendment to the military appropriations bill. No one knows what the ramifications of this action will be in the next year as military, CIA and government officials may be held responsible for treatment of prisoners.

Then for strike three, the New York Times (trying to regain its respect after Judith Miller) breaks a secret that the NSA is spying on citizens. I imagine the President will want to find out who told this secret but unlike the Valerie Wilson matter, this time you can be sure he means it.

The Times sat on the story for a year and picked the week the President was dreaming about to break the story that has dramatic implications. Our guess is that politicians are going to be the last ones to authorize this spying. They know about FBI Chief Hoover blackmailing Kennedy and could only envision President "Hillary" getting even with Republicans and the Monica Adventure and knowing everything about their private lives.

If that was not enough, one hour before the President's talk last night CBS's Sixty Minutes puts on a CIA manager who more or less said sure we send people all over the world to be tortured by boiling and other things. This was followed by a Katrina story we reported on at the time about New Orleans people trying to walk to safety being stopped by surrounding communities with shotguns. Not exactly the opening act I would want if I were President Bush.

When you attack someone you can expect them to return the favor. For years the Republicans and their attack dogs have been blasting the Networks and leading newspapers. This response should not have been unexpected.

And for better or worse, the battle will only intensify.

## YOU DON'T HAVE TO GET UP EARLY FOR THIS SPECIAL: WAL-MART HAS POVERTY ON SALE 365 DAYS A YEAR
## DECEMBER 21, 2005

Don't Miss This Opportunity to Fill Your Home with:

- *Living Wages 50% Off!*

- *Health Insurance Reduced to new low levels (But Supply is Limited)!*

- *Survival of Suppliers (Come Early, Work Hard and Stay Late)!*

- *Rebate on ALL USA made products you can find in the store Good Luck!*

We know it is not fair to blame our labor and economic problems on Wal-Mart but they certainly are responsible for leadership in the growing cutthroat business attitude in the USA. They used to promote that their products were made in the USA, but now almost all the merchandise is imported made by low cost labor from all over the world. They showed how to make more money by forcing low wages and minimum fringe benefits on their employees.

And they did it so well that today they are the role model for how corporations should make money and pay the management tens of millions of dollars a year. The result is the disappearance of our Manufacturing Base and the middle class jobs that has driven our economy for decades.

Corporations that pay higher wages like Ford and GM are fighting to stay out of bankruptcy. If they do, we as citizens will probably take over their pension obligations and someone else will take over the plants and you can expect the pay to be cut by 50%. Health insurance will be gone with the wind.

---

One thing will be true. Anyone and everyone could see this coming. Corporations could have changed this trend but took the easy way out by just worrying about their stock price and bonuses. Our politicians either did nothing or sold out to the international corporations. Maybe they have a plan on how this will all work out. I hope so. Life is not going to be pleasant as one organization after other battles to run from their obligations to their workers and cut wages, jobs and benefits.

The New York Transit Strike is a symptom of this trend and we can expect some future strike scenes to be right out of the 30's

P.S. One bright note: if you suddenly find yourself working short hours and at half your regular wages at least you have time to listen to that great MP Player you bought at a bargain price at well you know, where else!

# Afterword

I hope you enjoyed this series of Political Updates and that it helped you relive this exciting period in our political history. It's surprising to me how relevant the subjects still are today.

No one could match the humor, astute observations and writing skills of Mike Royko, but I graduated from an excellent Journalism School, the University of Illinois and had Professors who thought that my analysis and commentaries were pretty good. For example I got A's and B's from Professor Quincy Howe, the former CBS News Anchor and our nation's top war correspondent in World War II. So, it continued to be planted in my mind that maybe… someday I could be… just a little like Mike.

After service in the Army, I entered industry and not journalism, so there was no one to "dazzle "with my political views or complain about my observations. And so it remained for many years.

But when Mike died at an early age in 1997, I along with hundreds of thousands of followers missed his daily commentaries and observations about our city, nation and of course ourselves. I started writing some columns for my own enjoyment and then shared them with a few brave friends and relatives. They were written in a few minutes whenever I had some time.

Well that went on for a few years until some friends made the mistake in complimenting me…and even more important I got a computer at home that made it easy to share my observations with a "larger audience of really brave people".

So today although hundreds of Updaters read these commentaries I still basically write them for myself.  And the best part is that many Updaters respond to the commentaries and that it inspires them to voice their views on the subject …because that was the great value of Royko's columns. He made us think and discuss important matters facing our city and nation.

Mike was my inspiration… but unfortunately he's no longer here to guide us.

---

If you would like to contact Marvin or receive
the current  Political Updates please
email him at *marvin@mydonquixote.com*

---

# About the Author

Marvin Klein is the founder of PortionPac Chemical Corporation headquartered in Chicago. In 1964, PortionPac pioneered high concentrate detergent formulations, portion control packaging and environmentally sustainable programs. Dozens of concepts from safer chemicals to color-coded products and formal Janitorial education were introduced to the cleaning industry through PortionPac.

His goal has been to improve the effectiveness of cleaning on health and productivity while reducing environmental impact. Many of his business concepts were formed by outstanding high school teachers at Proviso High School and professors at the University of Illinois. After graduation he worked for the Ekco Product Company before service as an Army Intelligence Officer. Since 1956, he has worked in the janitorial, food service and corrections industries to improve professionalism, safety and recognition for Janitorial and Food Service Workers.

He is proud of his contribution to many organizations including the Child Nutrition Foundation, The Chicago Manufacturing Center and is currently on the Boards of the Healthy Schools Campaign, The John Howard Association for Prisoner Rights and The Compression Institute.

Marvin has written dozens of industry related articles and his previous books include: "It's Time to Be an Idealistic Environmental Capitalist", co-authored with Karen Wan; "Don't Go into Business to Make Money, There Are So Many Better Reasons" and "Put Junior to Work".

Marvin and his wife Bobbie have been married for 60 years and have three children and five Grandchildren.

They have been blessed.

# Acknowledgments

Well I have to start by thanking my Father. Where many parents shield their children from the difficult news of the world, my Father made sure we understood what was going on. Every night we listened on the radio to H. V. Kaltenborn and his analysis of the news and of course to key events like President Roosevelt's Fire Side Chats.

But he also made us listen to our country's biggest hate monger, Father Coughlin. It's like some parents who listen to every Cub game, of course the kids are going to become baseball fans...we had an exposure to politics, hatred and world affairs.

When it came to wars, corruption and Congress, my Father discussed the matter with us. And since my Father lost his arm in France during World War I, was active in Veteran's affairs and was an Adjudicator for the Veteran's Administration my brother, sister and I probably understood more about the dangers our country faced than most children.

Next in line to thank is our daughter Marsha who surprised me with a gift in 2006 by putting all the Updates that were in electronic format into a book. They are the Updates that are in this book. The people who read her book seemed to find it interesting so this idea has been brewing a long time.

Many thanks to Karen Wan for supporting this project just as she has by coauthoring "It's Time to Be an Idealistic Environmental Capitalist" and encouraging me to write "Don't Go Into Business To Make Money" and "Put Junior to Work" It is a pretty interesting mix of subjects: the Environment, Business, Raising Children and now Political Commentary. You can find them all on Amazon.

And if you like the covers and layout of my book as much as I do you certainly appreciate the skills of Ryan Roghaar, the artist that brought all my books to life. It would be hard to find anyone who is as creative and as easy to work with.

The Updates couldn't have survived for so many years without the support and encouragement of Bobbie, my wife of 60 years and our three children. Most husbands know that their key to success starts with a very understanding wife.

But my most important thank you is to the Updaters who have read, responded and reacted to the hundreds of Updates right up to the current time. They were the reason I wrote the Updates and your comments have made the project gratifying and educational for me. It has been an exhilarating exchange of ideas plus a lot of fun.

Finally, once again I want to thank Mike Royko for his genius and inspiration that influenced our nation.

Mike we miss you.